THE JEWISH SOUL ON FIRE

THE JEWISH SOUL ON FIRE

ESTHER JUNGREIS

William Morrow and Company, Inc.
New York 1982

Library of Congress Cataloging in Publication Data

Jungreis, Esther.
   The Jewish soul on fire.

   1. Family—Religious life (Judaism) 2. Orthodox
Judaism—United States. 3. Jungreis, Esther.
4. Jews—United States—Biography. I. Title.
BM723.J86   296.7'4   81-16994
ISBN 0-688-00955-7   AACR2

Printed in the United States of America

First Edition

1 2 3 4 5 6 7 8 9 10

ACKNOWLEDGMENTS

I have undertaken to write this book as a labor of love, for my purpose was not only to communicate ideas, but to touch hearts, enrich lives, and above all, to sanctify the Name of G-d. Therefore, I pray that those who read this book will perceive that each word was written in sincere devotion from the depths of my soul in the hope that all may find blessing therein.

I wish to express my deep-felt gratitude to my dear and revered parents, Rabbi and Rebbetzin Abraham Jungreis, who have been my strength and inspiration throughout my life. May the Almighty grant them length of days and much joy from all their children; to my wonderful husband, Rabbi Meshulem Halevi Jungreis, who, from the beginning, gave me the courage and incentive to write and was always there to advise me and to spur me on; to Barbara Janov, my most devoted friend and executive director of *Hineni*, who never lost patience as the manuscript had to be typed and re-typed, and whose forbearance and encouragement were a great source of strength to me; to my brothers, Rabbis Jacob and Benjamin Jungreis, who were always available to share with me their recollections of our childhood as well as the details of our internment in the concentration camps; to Bill Adler, my literary agent, who proved to be a genuine friend and who never lost faith in the book; to Hillel Black, editor in chief at William Morrow, whose guiding insights were of invaluable help and whose warmth and kindness fortified me; and last but not least, to my precious children, Chaya Sora and her husband Shlomo, my grandchildren Yosef Dov and Sirele, to my son Yisroel, my daughter Slava Chana, and my son Osher Anshil. They all sustained and encouraged me, and it is with blessing that I dedicate this book to them.

Rebbetzin Esther Jungreis

CONTENTS

AUTHOR TO READER

I WAS BORN at a difficult period. The winds of war were blowing over Europe, and although the Germans had not yet invaded our city of Szeged, the second largest city in Hungary, persecution of Jews had become an everyday happening.

My father was the Rabbi of our community. To him, the rabbinate was more than a profession, and even more than a calling—it was a legacy bequeathed by our ancestors who, for generations and generations, had all been rabbis.

From the time that I can recall, our house was a hub of activity, people coming and going, seeking relief from their many burdens and sorrows. Even the cab drivers at the railroad station knew our address, and automatically brought Jewish refugees to our residence. Deportations to the concentration camps had not yet begun, but the Hungarian authorities drafted all Jewish young men for slave labor, and since many of the transports passed through our city, our home became a temporary sanctuary for the homeless. The superintendent of our building had to be paid off regularly so that he would not report their presence to the police.

Every morning, I would awaken to the fragrant aroma of fresh bread and cake baking in the oven. My mother's sweet humming would be audible from the kitchen, and I would eagerly jump out of bed to help her prepare the table for our many guests. When my father returned from synagogue there were always people accompanying him, some of whom had stayed the night.

My mother would greet them at the door: "Come, breakfast is waiting." And even as she spoke, my father intoned the ancient blessing that preceded our partaking of food: "Let us lift our hands in sanctity and bless the L-rd."

My mother was a woman of great beauty, with sparkling black eyes, rosy cheeks, and a quick, flashing smile, but she was totally oblivious to her appearance. Her entire life revolved around the needs of others, nothing else mattered to her.

"What your mother can accomplish in minutes, others cannot do in days," my father would proudly tell us. Indeed, her energy knew no bounds, no task was too difficult or menial for her. As soon as our guests were seated, she approached each one of them to inquire whether they had laundry or mending. Without fuss or commotion, she would quickly ready everything and prepare packages of cakes and cookies which she would place in their knapsacks before they left.

The young men who came to our home had to wear yellow armbands which identified them as Jews, the lowest echelon of society. In those days, all Jewish males of military age were conscripted for labor battalions, which very often meant death. Szeged was their stopover, and my parents were determined that our home become their home, if only for a brief moment.

At our table, they were transformed. My father would open the Holy Books, and as they studied G-d's Word, their yellow bands of shame became badges of honor. Instead of slave laborers, they became soldiers of G-d, endowed with a special mission to kindle a Divine light in a world enveloped in darkness.

Alas, all too soon the clock would jar us back to reality, and as the young men prepared to leave, my father, his kindly face mirroring his anguish, would rise to his feet. Slowly and painfully, he would embrace each and every one of them. As he placed his hands upon their heads to invoke the priestly blessing, tears fell like raindrops into his beautiful long beard.

"May the L-rd bless you and keep you. May the L-rd make His Face shine upon you and be gracious unto you. May the L-rd turn His Countenance to you and give you peace."

My father would accompany them to the gate and stand there, whispering prayers until they turned the corner and disappeared from sight.

There was only one way for these boys to escape the transports, and that was to contract some contagious disease that would endanger the health of the non-Jewish combatants. We discovered that the injection of raw milk brought on a mysterious fever, and that a paste made from soybean powder smeared on the eyelids would simulate trachoma, but how to get these concoctions to the Jewish conscripts remained a formidable problem.

As the Rabbi of the community, my father had visiting rights to the detention camps, but he was always thoroughly searched, and therefore could not carry anything on his person. It was my mother who finally thought of a solution. She sewed pockets into the lining of my coat and secreted the precious potions there, together with some nourishing food and messages from home. Thus, at the age of six, I learned my first lesson in human responsibility: "You shall not stand idly by while the life of your brothers is in jeopardy" (*Leviticus* 19:16). To me, this was not a remote theoretical concept. Rather, it was a reality which challenged me every moment of the day. Along with this knowledge, I learned the meaning of Jewish pride, for despite the overwhelming risks and constant danger which this responsibility entailed, I also knew that I belonged to a people that demanded such commitment.

I remember our own deportation to Bergen-Belsen. En route, our transport was halted in Linz. They loaded us off the cattle cars, shaved our heads, and herded us into showers which we later realized were also gas chambers. I kept my eyes glued to the ground. I couldn't bear to look. I couldn't bear to see my beautiful, precious mother, whom I loved and respected, shorn of her dignity. I remember feeling that my life had come to an end. As young as I was, I somehow sensed that I was no longer a human being. And then, something strange occurred. As I was getting dressed, I put my hand into my pocket and felt a crumpled piece of paper. I took it out and unfolded it. It was a page from a prayer book. Unbeknown to me, my father had placed it there. On it was inscribed *Shema Yisrael*. It was only a torn piece of paper, but it told me that I was not alone, that my G-d lived. Slowly, I lifted my eyes.

Each day in Bergen-Belsen, when we were given our ration of stale bread, my father would hide a small piece. It is difficult even to conceive of the sacrifice and the risk this entailed, but my father, with superhuman will, would always manage to save a few precious crumbs so that we might have a Sabbath feast. My mother would collect these dry morsels and pretend that she was baking challah, and as the Sabbath approached, my father would gather us and gently cajole: "Close your eyes, my precious little ones. Close your eyes and make believe that we are back home. Mama has just prepared fresh challahs. The table is covered with a snowy white cloth. The candlesticks and the wine cups are glistening. There are angels all around us, the angels of the Sabbath."

As if by magic, the bread made from sawdust was transformed into sweet, crisp challah. Our tears became wine for sanctification, and the burning faith in our hearts became the candles of Friday night. Then, slowly, my father would hum the sweet melody of *Shalom Aleichem,* "Peace be unto you, ye angels of Sabbath, ye angels of G-d."

One Friday night, my little brother tugged at my father's sleeve. *"Tatie, tatie,"* he cried, "where are the angels, I do not see the angels."

Tears rolled down my father's cheeks and he answered in a quavering voice, "You, my precious children, are the angels."

As my father spoke, we stood more erect; our heads were held higher. G-d had bequeathed to us a precious gift which enabled us to soar upward, and, even if only for a fleeting moment, become angels of the Sabbath.

My feet were covered with sores and I was faint with hunger, but when I heard my father's voice, I somehow sensed that we would make it.

Prior to the Holocaust, there were more than eighty-five rabbis named Jungreis in Hungary. After the war, only a handful were left. My father was the only surviving son of my grandfather, and my brothers and I, the only surviving grandchildren. My many aunts and uncles, my little cousins, all perished in the flames. Only ashes remained.

When the war ended, we wanted more than anything else to settle in Israel, but the British granted only a small number of Jews entry. For two long, painful years we waited for visas in D.P. camps in Switzerland. Incredibly, during that time we were separated from our parents. I was assigned to a school near Montreux, while my brother was sent to a town near Zurich. Those years were perhaps the most miserable of all my existence. Having survived Hitler's hell, we longed to be a family again, but we were denied that simple wish. Every night, I cried myself to sleep and woke up in the midst of hideous nightmares which took me back to the concentration camps.

My parents couldn't bear to see our suffering, and decided that we would go to the first place that opened its doors to us. And so it was that we set sail for America on an Italian freighter. It took four long, grueling weeks to cross the Atlantic, and we arrived in the United States despondent and broken in spirit.

Then, miraculously, a message came to us from the past, a message that infused us with renewed determination and hope. It was a message from the ashes which would illuminate our path in the new land. This message came from my grandfather of blessed memory, the Rabbi of Nadudvar, Rabbi Yisroel Halevi Jungreis, who perished in the crematorium of Auschwitz.

Before he was deported, my grandfather collected all the sacred vessels of his synagogue and buried them in the courtyard. The Germans, however, in their typical methodical manner, dug deep in the earth to uncover any objects that the Jews might have hidden there. They found and took everything that my grandfather had so lovingly buried, everything, that is, except a single Sabbath candelabrum. When the nightmare passed, a survivor of the congregation found it and swore not to rest until it was returned to its rightful heirs. And so, it happened that shortly after our arrival in the United States, the candelabrum reached the trembling hands of my father.

My father's beard was now white. The deep furrows on his brow testified to the unspeakable horrors that he had experienced, but his eyes remained the same, full of compassion and kindness.

"My children," he said, "it is written in the ancient books that if all our people would observe but one Sabbath, the Messiah would come. This, then, must become our task, to teach our people to kindle the Sabbath lights. That is why we have survived."

I was struck by an awesome truth. The Sabbath had enabled us to retain our sanity in Bergen-Belsen, and now it would once again show us the way in our new home. The Nazis may have destroyed everything, but they could not destroy the Sabbath. The lone candelabrum had survived, and we pledged to continue to kindle the light. Perhaps, I thought, it was for this, that of all our treasures, only the candelabrum remained.

Many years later, when my youngest daughter was born, I named her after my grandmother, Slava Chana, who was the last to have kindled the lights of that candelabrum, and it was on that occasion that my father presented it to me.

"Now," he said, "that there is a living Slava Chana, the candelabrum belongs to you."

And today, seventeen years later, Slava Chana, together with her sister Chaya Sora, and her brothers Yisroel and Osher Anshil, all named after grandparents who perished in the flames, have proved themselves worthy of that trust. They are living testimony that the Covenant of our G-d continues to be fulfilled.

> This is My Covenant with them, saith the L-rd,
> My Spirit that is upon thee, and My words which
> I have put in thy mouth,
> shall not depart out of thy mouth,
> nor out of the mouth of thy seed,
> nor out of the mouth of thy seed's seed,
> saith the L-rd, from henceforth, forevermore.
>
> (*Isaiah* 59:20, 21)

This promise is the eternal bond between the Jewish people and their Creator, and because of it, I now lift my pen, so that the Covenant may continue to live on in the hearts of all children, so that the light which shone for our fathers may once again spread its rays and bring hope and strength to this generation.

one

ೱ

HERE I AM

My GRANDFATHER, five generations back, was the renowned Rabbi of Csenger, better known in rabbinic circles by the title of his monumental book, the *Menuchos Osher,* an exposition on the Torah. He assumed his pulpit in the late 1700's and served his people for more than forty years. His wisdom, piety, and saintliness made him a legend in his own time, and people flocked to him from every part of Hungary to seek his blessing.

In the same city of Csenger where my grandfather resided, there lived a wealthy baron who was a vicious anti-Semite. It happened that one day, his only son became deathly ill. The baron called in the finest physicians, but to no avail, the child did not respond.

Now, one of the maidservants in the baron's household had at one time been in the employ of a Jewish family, and she recalled how they would speak with awe of the "Miracle Rabbi." Having exhausted all possibilities, the baron decided to temporarily put aside his aversion to Jews and consult him.

The miracle occurred, the child was cured, and as an expression of gratitude the baron offered a handsome reward. My *zeide,* however, refused to accept any payment.

Instead, he requested the baron to extend kindness to all Jews, and demand the same from his descendents.

Generations later, in the early years of World War II, my father did a great deal of traveling, visiting young men who were detained in labor battalions. These trips were fraught with danger, and we always waited fearfully until my father returned home.

On one occasion, a gang of *zsandars*, Hungarian Gestapo, surrounded him and started to slap him around. Suddenly, a Hungarian army officer appeared and demanded to know what was going on. He looked at my father's identification papers and told the *zsandars* that he would take care of this "dirty Jew" himself. He threw my father into his car and brought him home to us unharmed. Only when they reached our house did he reveal that he was a descendent of the Baron of Csenger.

The stories about the *Menuchos Osher* are legion. His saintliness and piety knew no bounds. Every morning, before starting his prayers, he would send eighteen guilden, an enormous sum in those days, to Israel to build and maintain Torah communities. No sooner did someone make a contribution but that he would send it off. As a child, I never tired of hearing stories about him, but perhaps the tale that left the greatest impact on my life was about the dream my grandfather had on his Bar Mitzva night. In that dream, he found himself alone in the center of the synagogue. Suddenly, four strangers appeared in the four corners of the room. Instantly, he recognized them. They were the patriarchs, Abraham, Isaac, and Jacob, and the prophet Elijah. Overwhelmed by what he saw, he started to tremble. Whom should he greet first? he wondered. Should he go to Father Abraham, who bestowed upon us the legacy of charity and kindness? Should he go to Isaac, who taught us service and sacrifice, or should he go to Jacob, who symbolized Torah learning and wisdom? Or should he perhaps first greet Elijah, the prophet of good tidings?

But even as he was weighing these considerations, he recalled the teachings of the prophets.

"Elijah shall come unto you, and he shall turn the hearts of the fathers to the sons, and the sons to the fathers (*Malachi* 3:24) . . . Happy is he who sees him in his dreams and extends to him greetings, and is greeted by him in return . . ." (Saturday night liturgy, Prayer Book).

Immediately, my grandfather's dilemma was resolved. First he would greet Elijah, and then Abraham, Isaac, and Jacob in turn, for although he was only a young man, his perception was already that of a sage, and he understood that the heritage of the patriarchs could only take root in the hearts of parents and children who were united by love.

And so, in a dream on the day of his Bar Mitzva, the *Menuchos Osher* beseeched Elijah the prophet to teach him the secret through which he could bring blessing into the homes of our people.

His wish was granted, and his fame spread far and wide. Throughout his lifetime, he was known as the *Tzaddik*, the righteous one of Csenger, who made miracles come about for his people.

This passion to help others was passed on by the *Menuchos Osher* to his descendents, and as a small child I would listen in fascination as my father unraveled the most complex problems and brought peace and blessing to families.

Today, as this commitment has been passed on to me, and as the burdens of our people have increased, I often think of that special gift of my forefathers. I know in my heart that if I have helped liberate young people from the enslavement of cults, if I have helped husbands and wives find a measure of understanding, if I have reunited children with their parents, and if I have contributed to awakening a dormant generation to reclaim its heritage, I have done so only through the merit of my forefathers, and even as I write this book, I beseech their blessing. May they intercede on my behalf at G-d's Holy Throne so that He may grant me the words with which to unlock hearts and touch souls. In all my prayers, I have never asked for much more, but that I might be privileged to sanctify His Holy Name by helping our people come home.

I realize that in a secular world, such commitment is not so readily understood. Fortunately for me, however, the Almighty in His mercy spared my parents, granted me a husband who is also a descendent of the *Menuchos Osher,* and blessed me with four children who share this commitment; and so, I was never much bothered by those who failed to understand. My family always inspired and strengthened me, and in face of insurmountable difficulty, gave me the courage to go on.

Looking back on my early childhood years, I have often wondered how we managed to emerge from that Nazi hell with our sanity intact. I'm not only referring to our internment in Bergen-Belsen, but to the experiences that preceded it as well: the German occupation, the ghettos, and the deportations.

I had just started first grade when I was hit by the realization that the roof was caving in. I remember the day vividly. I came home from school, ran up the stairs, and called out, "Mommy, I'm home."

There was no response. The house was silent. Alarmed, I ran into the kitchen, where I found my mother crying.

"Mommy, what happened?" I asked, my heart skipping a beat.

For the longest time, my mother just looked at me as if she couldn't bring herself to speak. "Please, mommy," I begged, "what happened?"

"The Nazi *rashoim,* evil ones, have come. They are bent

on killing all of us," my mother answered, her voice conveying the anguish of our tormented people.

"G-d forbid!" I heard my father's voice in the background. "Why are you telling the child such terrible things?" he chided gently.

But my mother, who to this day is noted for the surgical precision with which she cuts to the truth, simply answered, "There's no sense in hiding the facts. She'll have to find out sooner or later."

It was March, 1944. The Nazi occupation of our city had begun. Each day, new edicts were passed against us, and my mother's words echoed ominously in my mind. All Jews had to be registered . . . Jewish children could not go to school . . . Jewish assets were frozen . . . Jewish businesses and properties were taken over . . . Jews were forbidden to travel . . . Jews had to wear yellow stars of identification . . . Jews were arrested without charges—some never to come home, some to be returned dead . . . Jews had to give up their apartments and were relocated . . . etc., etc.

Throughout that period, the Nazis played a clever psychological game. They kept insisting that they only wished for us to work. They put placards up all over, "*Arbeit macht frei*"—"Labor liberates." None of us believed it, but then again, we didn't believe the truth, either.

I remember one night when a heated discussion took place in our home. Someone from our community had met a Jew who had escaped from Poland and told grisly tales of our people being gassed and thrown into burning ovens. This, even my mother refused to believe. The Germans could never get away with such demonic savagery. After all, there was still a civilized world out there. And so, the story was attributed to the poor man's loss of sanity.

But whether we chose to believe it or not, there was nothing much that we could have done. We had no arms, and we had no place to run. The Hungarians were no less zealous in hunting us down than the Germans, and that great outside world that was supposed to come to our aid was silent. We were doomed.

The progression of evil that fell upon us kept escalating. No sooner did we accustom ourselves to our wretched lives in the ghetto than we were awakened one night by shouts and screams. They broke open our door and ordered us to get ready and out.

We were marched off to a brick factory at the outskirts of town. For two nightmarish weeks, they kept us there without hygienic facilities, sleeping in filth, literally on the ground. When they had finally gathered all the Jews they wanted, they took us off to the railroad station. As we marched, the local citizens came out to give us a send-off, some to gape, others to jeer. Suddenly, I heard loud laughter. I looked around and saw that the Nazis had provided the good Hungarian citizens with some sport. The Jewish patients from Szeged's psychiatric hospital were on exhibition. Locked in a cage as in a zoo, deranged from hunger, covered with filth and their own excrement, they had been put on display as proof of the subhuman Jew. They threw bits of food, bones, and garbage into the cage and rocked with laughter as those poor souls scrambled to catch it.

Those were my last memories of the city where I was born, Szeged.

My parents, my two brothers, and I, together with countless others, were shoved into a cattle car, and our long dark journey to Bergen-Belsen began. It was May, 1944.

For eight long months, we lived in the hell of that German concentration camp, and when the war ended in '45, we spent two more years in D.P. camps in Switzerland. In the winter of 1947, we arrived in New York City to begin a new life. I was almost twelve, and I was back in first grade trying to take up where I had left off that day so long ago when I came home from school in Szeged. In one year I went from the first grade to the seventh, and then to the eighth grade of the *yeshiva.*

I barely spoke English, but somehow I managed, and incredibly enough, won the school's essay contest. The reward was five pounds of chocolates, and my brothers and I had our first taste of the simple American delight of having all the candy we could eat.

As I became acclimated to my new life, I also became aware of the terrible disparity between the *yeshiva* in which I studied and the neighborhood where I lived. At school, everyone was committed to Jewishness; in my neighborhood, everyone was Jewish, but no one was committed. I was determined to close the gap. I would come home from school and run out to find the kids. And so it was that my first classes in Judaism were held on the stoops of East Ninety-third Street.

I couldn't bear to see the deprivation. Why should only the few be entitled to our heritage? Why shouldn't all our people be enriched by it? I invited my new-found friends to discover the world of the *yeshiva,* to participate in the religious youth organization in which I had become active, and above all, I invited them to our home to meet my mother and father.

In 1953, I went to Israel to study and teach. Shortly after my return in 1955, I married my fifth cousin, Rabbi Meshulem Halevi Jungreis. My husband's Hebrew name means "complete," and I believe that is the best way that I can describe him. He is a *complete* person.

As a young *yeshiva* student, he was known as a Torah giant whose brilliance was exceeded only by his compassionate heart. He, too, survived the concentration camps, and is the only one left from his family. His father was the Rabbi of the city of Gyongyos, and was reverently called by the title of his book, *Zachor V'Shamor*, a classic study on the meaning of the Sabbath. His five brothers, all in the rabbinate, and his two sisters, both married to rabbis, are all gone.

Given his many talents, my husband could have entered almost any profession, but we were both determined to follow in the path of our fathers and continue in the rabbinate. This, despite the onerous difficulties, the pain, and the constant sacrifice which we knew went with being an Orthodox rabbi in modern day America.

As a small child, I heard a story about a rabbi who visited America. Upon his return, he was asked about the quality of Jewish life in the New World. The rabbi thought for a moment, and then, half in jest, said, "In America, even the stones are *treife*, unkosher."

What the rabbi meant was that there were elements in American culture that were antithetic to the religious life. In the ensuing chapters, I shall comment on these schisms in detail, but in the interim, just consider the difficulty of teaching a religion that demands constant discipline and vigilance to men and women who are accustomed to unbridled freedom. Why should they willingly embrace laws and rituals which are burdensome and restrictive?

Or consider the rabbi who must touch a man's conscience if he is to elicit greater religious commitment. How is he to achieve this in a society which idealizes happiness and associates guilt with neurosis? Why should people allow him to make them feel guilty? And finally, in a democracy where everything is voted upon, what is there to preclude people from voting out religious laws that are not to their liking?

These were only a few of the difficulties that we had to overcome. Not to mention that in the rabbinate we would have a thousand and one bosses, each pulling in different directions, each seeking his own *koved*, status. Significantly, there is a popular joke that to be an Orthodox rabbi is not a job for a nice Jewish boy!

Yet we would not forsake the tradition of our fathers, and willingly took upon ourselves the mantle of the rabbinate. After having occupied pulpits in New Jersey and Long Island, we gathered a small group of dedicated friends, and in 1963, established the first Orthodox synagogue in North Woodmere, Long Island. At that time, Jewish suburbia was a spiritual wasteland, and people were embarrassed by open manifestations of Jewishness. A Reform or Conservative temple might succeed, but an Orthodox synagogue, we were told, didn't have a chance. We had to find novel ways to attract people, and as always, my mother came to our aid. For every Sabbath, she prepared a gourmet Jewish feast: kugel, cholent, kishke, gefilte fish. "Come for lunch," I would invite, and only later did I say, "But first we'll go to synagogue." We were not content, however, with just getting people to pray. More than that, we wanted them to become learned, to understand "why."

My husband began to teach the men, but how to involve the women remained a problem. As the mother of four children, I soon found a way. Women with small children would do almost anything to be relieved of their burdens for a few hours a day. And so, we started "Tiny Tots." I would teach the little ones (with my own four constantly present), while my husband taught the parents in an adjacent room. Soon homes were becoming kosher, and there were Jews attending synagogue, not for lunch, but because it was Sabbath.

Educating the older children was not quite so simple. The parents were willing enough to send the boys who had to be prepared for Bar Mitzva, but the girls did not have the same pressure. Having been raised in a home where girls were considered of utmost importance, I couldn't bear to see this neglect, for more than boys, it is girls who, as mothers of our people, are the custodians of the future.

And that's how I started a class in my kitchen. As I

folded the laundry, prepared dinner, or held a little one on my shoulder, I would tell stories of our ancient past, stories of the glorious women by whose merit our forefathers were saved from Egypt, stories of prophetesses, and of women who, at Mount Sinai, were the first to accept the Torah.

"Promise me that you will never forget, that you will continue," I would beg my girls.

Many years have passed since those early days, but every once in a while I get a phone call from a girl who says, "Rebbetzin, I haven't forgotten. I just became a mother. Please come to my *simcha*, celebration."

It was my husband who urged me to expand my activities, to reach beyond the confines of our synagogue. "G-d gave you the gift of speech. You must try and reach the people in every community," he insisted. The children were small, and I wouldn't leave them with a sitter, so once again my dear mother came to the rescue.

"You go," she agreed with my husband. "I will stay with the children."

And so it was that I started to speak for schools, organizations, synagogues, and community centers.

One summer we were vacationing in the Catskills, when we met Rabbi and Mrs. Sholom Klass, who had just started to publish the Jewish Press.

"If you want to carry an excellent column," my husband told them, "ask my wife to write it!"

The whole thing seemed ridiculous to me. What did I know about writing for a paper? But with my husband's prodding, I also started that. We were considering what to call the column, and since I found it regrettable that in America the title "Rebbetzin," rabbi's wife, had lost its luster, I decided to do something about it. For the most part, my fellow rebbetzins resented the title, but I, who loved the rabbinate, took pride in it. I dreamt of the day when Jewish life would be so accepted that little girls would want to play, not only nurse, teacher, or actress, but rebbetzin as well. So we called the column "The Rebbetzin's Viewpoint," and if today, twenty years later, the title has some cachet, I'm grateful for it.

In 1972, during the week that my eldest son, Yisroel, was to be Bar Mitzvaed, I received an invitation to address a convention of college students. Normally, I would have immediately accepted, but under the circumstances, I just didn't see how I could manage. Yisroel's Bar Mitzva was to take place on Labor Day, and the convention was scheduled for that weekend.

But the family wouldn't hear of my not going. They convinced me that we could work out the preparations and I would have ample time to get back.

A few hundred students gathered for the convention, and as I spoke, I felt a surge of anger. "Why don't you do something?" I challenged. "You condemn those who were silent when six million were taken to the gas chambers, but today millions more are dying, and you just sit there! Look about you. People are disappearing in assimilation, alienation intermarriage. You have a powerful organization behind you and yet you remain indifferent."

"Well, what can we do?" the students asked, throwing the ball right back into my lap.

"Why, if I had your organizational clout," I replied, "I would take Madison Square Garden and call for a Jewish happening. I would tell everyone that it's time to wake up, that we have become an endangered species, and if we want our people to survive, we must become Jews again."

The students were fired with the idea, and right then and there they endorsed it. But being familiar with organizational life, I also knew that no sooner would the convention end and the releases be given to the papers, than the entire matter would be over and done with.

But a few days later, at my son's Bar Mitzva, one of my

friends jokingly announced the Madison Square Garden program. Without even consulting me, he invited those present to my house so that we might start the ball rolling. I smiled to myself, convinced that it would never be. G-d knows, I had enough responsibilities without looking for additional burdens. But that which is meant to be happens despite your will and desire, and incredibly, the next night a group showed up at my house to plan what we laughingly called "the Jewish event of the century."

One of the men pointed out that since the Jewish community was very polarized, with one group vying with the other, it would be best to form a new umbrella movement.

"Call it *Hineni*, 'Here I am,'" Morty suggested, and the recommendation was readily accepted.

Hineni is the Biblical term with which all the great prophets of Israel responded to G-d's challenge. Abraham, Isaac, Jacob, Moses, Samuel, Isaiah, Jeremiah, all affirmed their faith with "*Hineni*, Here I am, totally committed to the service of G-d and man."

I loved the name, it expressed my beliefs, but frankly, I still did not regard any of it seriously.

One of those present at the meeting was Barbara Janov (today *Hineni's* international executive director, and my dearest personal friend). Barbara was at that time president of the United Parent-Teachers' Association of the Board of Jewish Education of New York. I had spoken at one of her educational luncheons, met her once or twice later, and by chance, she came that night to my house. She was immediately taken with the idea, and wouldn't let go until we went to the Garden to explore it further.

It was no small matter to translate such ambitious dreams into reality. The Garden was a first. It had never been done before. We had no precedent to follow, but I guess that G-d wanted it to happen, and things miraculously fell into place.

I panicked a million times. I had terrible visions of an

empty house, of standing up there and not being able to speak, of being booed, jeered, and heckled. But throughout these terrible nightmares, my family kept insisting that everything would be okay.

But what I would say, and how to fill the Garden, I had yet to discover. There was only one thing of which I was certain. If I were to succeed, I would need G-d's special blessing. I remembered my studies in Jewish history, and now tried to make its lessons work for me. It is written that the Holy Temple in Jerusalem was destroyed only because of strife between brother and brother, and it is written that it will be rebuilt when we become united as one. I was determined somehow to reach for that miracle and get as many people as possible to work together. I contacted every school and organization, and invited them to participate by setting up information booths in the Garden lobby in a program which I called "a Smorgasbord of Jewish Ideas." At every booth a specific concept would be projected, literature given out, and questions answered. Upon entering the Garden, each person would be handed a *Hineni* shopping bag, and as they made their way through the lobby, they would discover the world of Jewish ideas.

Then I asked my dear father to go with me to his friends and colleagues, the sages of our generation, so that I might go fortified with their blessings.

On November 18, 1973, we opened at the Felt Forum of Madison Square Garden. I was waiting in my dressing room when my father came to tell me that crowds were standing outside and couldn't get in.

"You must do something, my child," my father said. "They must be allowed to participate."

Barbara explained that the rules in the Garden were very strict, and since all the seats had been filled, it would create a fire hazard to let more people in.

But my father was right. We could not allow anyone to be turned away. I asked to speak to the floor manager, but he remained adamant. The aisles and the floor must be kept clear, and only those holding tickets would be allowed to enter.

"You believe in G-d?" I asked him.

"I haven't missed church on Sunday yet," he said matter of factly, "but what does that have to do with it?"

"This is no ordinary event. It's not entertainment or a fun program. We have assembled our people for a specific purpose, to reaffirm G-d's Covenant. You know your Bible. Surely you know that we, the Jewish people, are bound by a promise to keep the Commandments and become a blessing to all mankind."

"What do you want me to do?" he asked in exasperation.

"Let them in," I said, "and I promise you that you will share in our history. One day, when you come in front of G-d's Throne, you will tell the story and you will receive your reward."

"I must be crazy for agreeing," he said with a sheepish grin, "but all right, let them in! They'll have to sit on the floor in front of the stage, though, and if they disturb you, don't blame me."

I was scared stiff, but I wouldn't let on. What if someone heckled me? Nevertheless, I knew that my father was right. Every person had to be allowed in.

The crowds were now making their way through the lobby, stopping at booths, asking questions, discovering. Inside the Garden, there was a true celebration. Jewish music was playing and everyone was dancing.

Suddenly, the music stopped, and I knew that the time had come for me to speak. There was a knock on the door, and there was Barbara, with the security people right behind her.

"It's more than we could ever have hoped for," she said,

her voice full of excitement. "Everybody is waiting for you. Go with *mazel*, luck."

We looked at one another and our eyes filled with tears. It had been a long, grueling year. There were days when we worked twenty-four hours and didn't get to sleep at all. Now, the moment had come, and I could only hope that we would be worthy of reaching the hearts of our people.

I had a sick feeling at the pit of my stomach. My mind went blank. What would I say to all those thousands of people? I forgot everything that I had planned. I looked around for my father, and as if he sensed that I was searching for him, he appeared at the end of the corridor and slowly made his way toward me.

"May angels of mercy accompany you, my precious child," he whispered as he placed his hands over my head in blessing. "May G-d give you the words with which to reach every heart."

The stage was pitch black. I searched in vain for some familiar face, but the spotlight hit me, and I felt blinded. I had never before spoken in total darkness. For a moment, I froze, and then I started to speak.

"You are a Jew . . . ."

I felt as if my heart had stopped beating. My voice quavered, but I mustered my courage and continued:

"You are a Jew. You have created civilizations. You have given birth to every ideal that has shaped mankind: Justice, peace, love, the dignity of man, have all had their genesis in your Torah. But above all, you have been given the unique mission of proclaiming the One-ness of G-d!

"You are a Jew. You have traveled the four corners of the earth. You have become a part of every people, and yet you have remained a people apart. You have known every form of oppression. Your body has been scorched by fire. You are weary, your spirits flag, your memory fails. You have forgotten your past, you cannot even recall your father's prayer.

"But there is one prayer, one little prayer that you do remember, a prayer that has been a beacon of faith throughout the centuries of darkness, a prayer that has brought you back to the faith of your ancestors, a prayer that speaks of your own mission in life: *'Shema Yisrael*—Hear, O Israel, the L-rd our G-d, the L-rd is One!' "

Suddenly, the entire audience repeated those immortal words. *Shema Yisrael* resounded throughout the Garden. The walls themselves seemed to tremble with the song of our people. It was a spontaneous affirmation of faith. Now, everyone was singing, "Hear, O Israel, the L-rd our G-d, the L-rd is One!"

Those who were there that night will never forget. It was not something that we could ever duplicate. It was the beginning of *Hineni,* the movement dedicated to awakening our Jewish people.

Madison Square Garden was the generator that spread currents throughout the country. From Miami to Vancouver, from Los Angeles to Toronto. From every city, they called, and in every city, the miracle reoccurred. Jews who had never identified with their people, who had never thought about their heritage, were returning home again.

"How do you do it?" people would ask. "Teach us your method."

It had never before occurred to me that I had any special method. I had never studied speech or taken lessons in drama. I was a Jew who believed in G-d, and I spoke from my heart. My father had always raised me according to the dictates of the sages: "Words that come from the heart must enter another heart." If you speak sincerely, the people will know and understand. You don't need any other talents.

And so, I guess that if there is any one method that can be attributed to me, it would be this directness. In my talks, I have never sugar-coated or camouflaged the truth, and often, as I spoke of our people, I would break down. There may have been those who were embarrassed by my tears, by my open manifestation of emotion, but I have never attempted to disguise my feelings. Live recordings of my speeches have caught these tears, and there have been those who suggested that, in production, I should cut them, but those tears are not my own. They belong to my people, and they shall remain.

A few weeks after Madison Square Garden, a woman called from Los Angeles. She desperately needed help for her daughter, who had become part of a cult, Jews for Jesus. Since at that time I was scheduled to speak at the Hollywood Palladium, I suggested that she bring her daughter there. But the girl, warned of my coming, never kept the appointment. Nevertheless, I didn't give up, I was determined to reach this child. I went to her home and waited into the early hours of the morning, but to no avail, she never appeared.

Finally, she agreed to meet with me, but when she arrived, she came fortified with her entire group and her non-Jewish minister alongside. They were looking for a confrontation, but I refused to comply. Religious debates are not to my liking, and I have never allowed myself to be drawn into them. I have always been of the conviction that since the faith we are born into is not of our choosing, G-d must have wished for some of us to be Jews, some Moslems, some Christians. To try to negate this by being a missionary would be a repudiation of His Will.

I have often explained my position by comparing the world to a great symphony in which each nation has been given its own unique instrument to play. As a Jew, it was my mission to preserve the song of my people and thereby prevent it from disappearing. And so, I had no intention of getting embroiled in an exchange with a Christian minister, but I did make a silent vow to teach that song to my children. The girl, however, refused to speak to me privately, and therefore, so far as she was concerned, my visit to Los Angeles ended in futility.

It was spring, and the holiday of Passover was coming upon us. As all Jewish housewives, I, too, was inundated with housecleaning, but the eyes of the girl from Los Angeles kept calling me.

Passover is the holiday of freedom, when the Almighty G-d brought us forth from bondage. How could I sit down at my Seder knowing that our children remained enslaved? I told Barbara that once again we must try, and so we flew off to L.A. that night.

I was speaking at a school when a local rabbi nervously informed me that the girl was there. She was giving out missionary leaflets in an attempt to convert Jewish children.

"Should we get rid of her?" he asked.

"Let her be," I answered. "As long as she stays and listens, that is all we need."

That night, I went to her home and once again waited. The minutes ticked by, it was 2:00 A.M., but still she did not come. Her parents retired, Barbara dozed off, and I remained awake in the darkness. Something told me that she would come home.

Suddenly, I heard the door open, and there she was, a frail child whose soul once stood at Sinai, but had now lost its way. I looked at her and I loved her. I wanted to clasp her in my arms. "I have been waiting for you," I said, "and your people have been waiting even longer. Here is the prayer book of your fathers. Let us open it and may G-d help us."

Two of us came to Los Angeles, Barbara and I. The next morning, when we left, we were three.

It never occurred to me to phone ahead or to ask my husband and children whether they would be willing to accept a new addition to our family. Nor did I consider consulting my eldest daughter, Chaya Sora, who, being the same age, would have to assume a large share of the responsibility. To her credit, Chaya Sora responded by greeting her with open arms. From Csenger, to Szeged, to New York, nothing had changed.

For two years, she lived with us, and we had the privilege of marrying her off from our home. Today, she is the mother of children, and she continues to sing that "Jewish Song."

The girl in Los Angeles was my first direct experience in reclaiming cult children, and since then there have been countless more. Each of them has his own unique story, and perhaps, one day, I shall recall them all. But one salient truth remains: The *pintele Yid*, that Jewish spark within the soul, can never evaporate.

Yes, Madison Square Garden was the generator through which waves spread, not only throughout the United States, but in Israel as well. The day after the Garden program, I was invited to the Israeli Consulate, where Consul Shlomo Levin presented me with a fascinating proposal.

Would I go to Israel and speak to the soldiers in the armed forces? I was dumbstruck. There was nothing on earth I would have liked better, but even as I yearned to go, I knew I would have to decline. Who was I to speak to those valiant soldiers? How dare I speak about Jewish destiny to those who actually put their lives on the line? It would have been wonderful, but no, I could never even consider it.

Nevertheless, despite my protestations, Shlomo Levin proceeded with his plans and sent Madison Square Garden publicity pictures to the Israeli Army Entertainment Corps.

I was in my office one morning, when Barbara told me that I had a call from Israel. Thinking that my son Yisroel (the Hebrew name for Israel) was on the phone, I picked up the receiver. The voice at the other end was heavily accented. "This is army headquarters in Tel Aviv calling. When can you come, and for how many performances?"

My voice choked in my throat. When could I come, and for how many performances? "I will come right away, I will speak the whole day," I almost shouted.

"Hey, *chevra*, guys," I heard the soldier shout at the other end. "You must hear this. This dame really believes in us, and she speaks Hebrew!"

Unbeknown to me, the soldiers thought I was a singer. Having received my Garden publicity pictures, they automatically assumed that I was an entertainer, but I, unaware of this misunderstanding, proceeded with my plans.

First, I called my parents, and my mother, true to form, immediately began to prepare packages for the soldiers. But I wanted to take something special, something that would convey our feelings of esteem and gratitude, something that would speak of our Jewishness. Shlomo Levin suggested that I take *kipot*, skullcaps. I thought he was putting me on. Being familiar with the anti-religious sentiment prevalent among many Israelis, I knew that *kipot* was one gift that was sure to bomb. But he kept insisting that I would be able to get away with it, and so I decided to give it a try.

In those days, jeans were just coming into vogue, and knowing the Israeli proclivity for everything American, Barbara and I decided to make *kipot* from blue denim, with the *Hineni* emblem sewn on them. We found someone to donate fabric, and my dear father enlisted some Chassidim to make them. The women of my sisterhood sewed on the emblems, and I felt very good about the whole thing. Just as in the Garden, we were once again contributing to a joint effort, and because of it, I felt confident that it would result in blessing.

However, there were still problems that had to be overcome. At large programs in the States, there was always music preceding my speeches, but where would I get a band to accompany me to the army camps? Even as I was wondering how to resolve the problem, a lawyer, who had heard me speak in Miami and whose hobby was music, called to volunteer his services. His sons and their friends had organized a terrific band, he informed me. True, they didn't know too many Jewish songs (they were just getting involved in Jewish life), but they were expert in jazz, and would consider it an honor to help.

We were an odd-looking bunch at Kennedy Airport. My musician friends came in full gear: rhinestone-studded tuxedos, and to prove their newfound Jewish convictions, they proudly displayed their *tzitzit*, ritual fringes worn by observant Jews.

My mother, true to her promise, met us at the airport with a truckload of *shmattas*, "hand-me-downs."

"Mama," I protested weakly, about to faint, "there is no way they will take this on the plane."

"Never mind," she insisted, "you're flying El Al. Just tell them it's for the soldiers of Israel."

Mama stood there and wouldn't budge until every package was placed on the conveyor belt, and to this day, whenever I go, mama brings her packages along. Year after year, I repeat my protests, but mama just stands there (all 4 feet, 11 inches of her), and somehow, the packages go through.

Our first program in Israel was scheduled at one of the largest air force bases. This time, I was truly nervous. My Hebrew was okay, but not nearly adequate for a major address. What's more, I had heard that Israeli soldiers were not inclined to politeness, and if they didn't like a program, it was not unusual for them to throw bottles or tomatoes. I had visions of myself being chased off the stage, splattered.

My first inkling that something was wrong should have come when the officer who was to escort us to the base asked what songs I liked to sing. I looked at him blankly, and surmised that I probably didn't understand his Hebrew slang. By the time we got to camp, the base theater was full. Word had gone out that a top American entertainer was coming, and the soldiers were anticipating a terrific evening. The jazz music was just what they'd hoped for, and they couldn't wait for me, "the singer," to start the show.

As frightened as I had been at Madison Square Garden, here I knew terror. I wanted to run, to forget the whole thing. But it was too late now.

The words of my father kept echoing in my mind: "Angels of mercy go with you, my precious child. G-d give you the words to reach every heart." If ever I needed a blessing, I thought, it was tonight.

I heard them announce my name. I had to get on stage. The applause was deafening. The soldiers were waiting for song and music.

"You are a Jew," I started to whisper in Hebrew. The soldiers looked at one another. There was an uncomfortable silence. I felt something was terribly wrong, but I didn't know what. No matter, I had to go on. I resigned myself to the worst, and waited for the heckling to start.

But no one made a sound. There was just that awful silence. I spoke for over an hour, and still no one moved. I looked out at the audience and saw their eyes. They were moist with tears, as were mine.

"Soldiers of Israel," I now asked, "why do you weep? You who, as the prophets of old, are swifter than eagles, stronger than lions. You who walk undaunted, unafraid, into fire, why do you weep? Can it be that dormant in your souls is that *pintele Yid*, that spark from Sinai that awakens you in the stillness of the night, that reminds you of your past, and of G-d's promise to bring you home to your land?"

When I finished, they stood as one. "*Kol ha kavod*, Hats off!" they cheered in true military style.

We gave out the *kipot*, but we didn't have nearly enough, and I realized that Shlomo Levin had been right. They had millions of questions and we stayed far into the night, talking, searching, tracing our way back to Sinai.

We were a new phenomenon that they couldn't quite handle. The soldiers were accustomed to a rabbinate that was somber and distant. In the army, religious programs were delegated to the chaplains, and only those who were observant attended. But I was invited by the entertainment corps, and therefore made contact with those who would normally never be exposed to religion. It was highly irregular, and it had never been attempted before. I didn't realize it, but I soon found out that there were political repercussions as well.

Early the following morning, we were visited by the officer in charge. He regretted very much, but he could not allow us to go on. He agreed that the soldiers were enthusiastic, but if I wished to continue, it would have to be under the auspices of the chaplaincy. This I did not want. There was no point in my speaking to those who were already committed to our Torah way of life.

The officer, however, was unbending, and explained that the matter was not in his hands. In Israel, religious people are organized into religious parties, and therefore there might be those who would view my programs as religious propaganda and electioneering!

"If I let you go on, I could lose my *falafel* (Hebrew slang for officer's bars)," he added half-jokingly.

"Look," I pleaded, "deep down in your heart, you know the truth. You know that what I said last night was more important than any form of entertainment. You know that to us, religion is not just a question of ritual and ceremonies. It is our very life, our very existence, and the reason why we are here in this land. Let me go on as scheduled," I begged, "and as far as you are concerned, you don't have to know that I'm not an entertainer. If anyone should say something, blame it on the Consul in New York. It was he who led you to believe that I was a singer."

He hesitated for a moment, paced back and forth,

seemed about to speak, and changed his mind again. It was obvious that he was torn. He wanted to help, but he was hesitant.

"I must be crazy for agreeing, but okay, have it your way. Only one thing . . . never mention my name! As far as I'm concerned, this meeting never took place."

I didn't see him again until just before our return to the States. I was speaking in Jerusalem, when I spotted him in the audience. The evening was over, we were about to leave, when he ran up to the stage with a package for me. It was a citation from the Israeli army, an expression of thanks, and I accepted it with trembling hands. I have received many awards in my life, from many organizations, but to me, that little plaque has always been the most precious.

Our tour was to have lasted two weeks, but the demand was such that we extended it to four. T.V., radio, newspapers, all covered us, from Jerusalem to Tel Aviv, to Sinai. From kibbutzim to moshavim, the message caught on, and I reaffirmed what I already knew. Embedded in the soul of every man is a great love for the Almighty G-d, and if there are those among us who have become cynical, who have lost their faith, it is only because of the brutality that surrounds us.

Our tradition teaches us that Jerusalem is the heart of the world, and therefore it was not surprising that the reverberations of our program were felt in every land. South Africa, Europe, Australia—from every continent invitations came, and overnight, *Hineni* became an international movement.

As our organization expanded, we soon realized that there was one area where every man was hurting, where he desperately needed guidance and help, and that was *family*.

What is G-d's prescription for raising children? What does the Bible say about becoming a better husband or wife? How do you find lasting happiness? How do you overcome fear and loneliness? How do you choose a proper mate? How do you create a stronger and more meaningful family life?

These were the real problems of today, and it was in these areas that we were determined to build. And so we established *Hineni* School, where every lesson in the Bible became a workshop in living, where we built a bridge from Sinai to the twentieth century.

"Turn it over again and again, search its pages, for everything is to be found in it" (*Ethics of the Fathers*, Chapter 5:25), is the advice of our sages, and indeed, those who attended our classes discovered that it was so. From the most trivial to the most complex problem, the solution was to be found in G-d's Book.

One of the people who took an interest in our program was Jackie Sloane. At thirty-two, Jackie was sitting on top of the world. Beautiful, bright, a leader of New York society, she could have lived her life in a whirlwind of partying, but Jackie was a serious person who regarded her family as her priority. She was fascinated by her newfound Biblical insights, and as she absorbed a lesson, she would immediately transmit it to her children and friends.

Jackie was one of those rare individuals who was never content to keep anything to herself. If she found something beautiful, something meaningful, she felt a need to share it with others. She wanted everyone to benefit, everyone to be enriched and find the lasting happiness that she had found. And so it was that one day, Jackie approached me with the idea of starting a class for her friends.

Our Manhattan chapter was soon established, and women who had hitherto found their pleasure in the Hamptons and Palm Beach discovered the lasting joy, the inner calm and tranquillity of a life linked to traditions and Biblical values.

As our program developed in scope, it became evident

that the quest for these Biblical truths was not limited to any one race, creed, or color, for family-related problems are the affliction of our entire generation, and all of us are desperately seeking for answers.

It is to these challenges that I shall address myself in the ensuing chapters, and I hope and pray that our timeless Biblical insights may bring blessing to all those who seek.

two

ɞ

ROOTS –
AN AMERICAN QUEST

ADJUSTING TO A NEW and alien environment entails a certain amount of culture shock and emotional turmoil, and our family's experience proved no exception. Perhaps one of the most difficult things for us to accept was the realization that, despite the freedom and opportunity offered in America, the great majority of our people chose to remain ignorant and uncommitted as Jews.

In 1947, my family moved into the East Flatbush section of Brooklyn, which was then predominantly Jewish, and yet devoid of all semblance of Jewishness. I remember my indignation when, one day, soon after our arrival, while walking with my father, some youngsters pointed to his long white beard, and called out, "Hey, look at Santa Claus!"

I couldn't believe that Jewish children could be capable of such insensitivity, but my father was quick to explain that they didn't know any better. They may have been Jewish, but they had no understanding of their religion, and most likely they had never come in contact with a rabbi who had a beard. To prove his point, my father asked them for their Jewish names.

The children became silent. Not one of them was able to answer. The irony of it all hit me. In the concentration camps, the Germans tried to destroy us by denying us our

45

names and calling us by numbers. But no matter what they did, our names, rooted in the Bible, remained imprinted on our souls. Even in the darkest hour, they could not deprive us of our identity, and yet, these Jewish children, growing up in the land of the free with every opportunity to claim their birthright, remained nameless.

"We must teach them," my father said urgently, recalling that our forefathers merited redemption from Egyptian bondage because they had retained their identity and never abandoned their Jewish names. "As long as we have a sense of ourselves, of our history," my father went on to explain, "there is no force on earth that can destroy us."

And from that day on, despite his limited English, my father found marvelous ways to reach these children. Whenever he left the house, his pockets were full of candies which he would distribute among the youngsters who eagerly waited for him. As soon as they saw my father approach, they would run to greet him. Proudly, they would call out their Jewish names (which they had by now learned), and recite the blessings which my father had taught them. On the Sabbath and on the holidays, they would gather in our home, sit at our table, and discover the beauty of our heritage. Strangely enough, despite a language barrier and a cultural and generation gap, my father, through his boundless love and wisdom, was able to touch their hearts and communicate with them as no one else could.

It took me quite a while to accustom myself to the rootlessness of the American Jew, but with the years, I came to understand it better. America was founded on dreams of the future, on innovation and change. Immigrants came to these shores determined to chart a course for a new and better tomorrow. What was old became archaic, what was new became synonymous with progress.

These cultural attitudes struck the Jewish people perhaps the hardest, for our religion is based upon respect for the past and reverence for all that is timeless. Therefore, it could not coexist with a philosophy that worshipped newness for its own sake, and regarded change as a cure-all for all problems. The situation was further compounded by the fact that the Jewish immigrants who came to this country prior to the Holocaust had precious few underpinnings to sustain them. They were mostly young men and women who had journeyed here to pave the way for their socially and financially depressed families. In their obsession with Americanization, they sacrificed everything that was reminiscent of the *shtetl,* small town European Jewish life. The beard, the *yarmulke,* the *tallis,* were all sources of embarrassment to them, but most tragic of all, Jewish education became the major casualty.

While much progress has been made since those early days, and religion is "in" today, a residue of that original attitude still remains, and I have often been confronted by it.

Some years back, I was invited to address a parlor meeting at the home of a prominent physician on Long Island. Among the many guests was a couple who arrived accompanied by their eighteen-year-old daughter. The girl, dressed in some outlandish garb, had an air of disdain about her, and it was obvious that she was present under pressure.

I hadn't said more than a few words, when she interrupted. "I just can't believe what I am hearing!" she exclaimed self-righteously.

"How can anyone talk about reclaiming souls in this day and age? Religion may have been necessary in the past, when man had to divest himself of his primitive instincts, but for heaven's sake, we have evolved, and today the only religion that is required is love."

For a moment, everyone was taken aback by her outburst. Then, one of the guests, a distinguished elderly gentleman, attempted to reason with her. "Don't you think, my dear, that a religion that is thousands of years old and has transcended civilizations is worth preserving, even today, in the twentieth century?"

The girl glared at him, not deigning to answer. Her look indicated that she considered him an old fool, and as if to confirm her thoughts, someone else explained that young people have their own way of looking at things, which the elderly cannot possibly understand.

As revolting as I found this girl's conduct, however, I was even more shocked by the apologetic attitude of the adults. Solely on the basis of her youth, she had managed to put down a roomful of distinguished individuals. There was no getting away from it. What had taken place reaffirmed that we live in a society in which being older is associated with senility and youth is symbolic of intelligence and worldliness.

"Tell me," I asked, "what is this 'progress' that you are talking about? What is this religion of love that you are advocating? Has love made your generation more compassionate, more humane? Has it brought peace to mankind, and has it, as you claim, divested man of his primitive instincts?

"I know that you would like to believe that through change and innovation all the tensions of the world can be resolved, but what about fallout, biological warfare, and ecological disaster? Are they not the products of progress?

"How far do you think evolution has brought you? Do you really believe that your ability to flick a switch grants you greater insight into the mysteries of life than Moses possessed? Do you think that the marvels of technology enable you to communicate more meaningfully than Isaiah? And more important, are you happier today than your grandparents were?"

I went on to explain to the girl that our religion has always been in conflict with the times. As a matter of fact,

Abraham was already out of step with his society, but neither he nor any of our people would ever have considered compromising their beliefs. Indeed, what would have happened to us, had they not stood firm? Where would we be today, if they had abandoned their heritage? We survived as Jews because we withstood the cultural pulls of every age, because we anchored our lives to concepts and values that are timeless.

"No," I said to her, "we are not impressed with your twentieth-century progress, nor do we seek anyone's endorsement. Judaism, I assure you, will survive long after the ideals that you espouse go out of style."

The girl was taken aback, and for a moment it appeared as though I had reached her; but her parents, interpreting my candor as a personal attack on their daughter, quickly came to her defense. "Come, let's go," they said indignantly, and with a smug smile on her face, the girl walked out with her parents.

I realized then that it was not only religion that had fallen victim to the deification of progress. Equally affected has been our manner of raising children.

Reverence for the past automatically inspires respect for parents and grandparents, but the celebration of youth has the opposite effect: Roles are reversed, and homes become child rather than parent centered. Soon after our arrival in this country, my mother observed this phenomenon and expressed alarm at the ill-mannered aggressiveness of American children.

One day, she returned from a shopping trip in a state of shock. She told us, "I was standing at the check out counter with my groceries, when this little boy started to whine and cry. When his mother refused to buy him what he desired, he pushed and kicked her, and she just stood there accepting his abuse as if it was the most natural thing for a child to hit his mother. How can you raise children in such an atmosphere?" my mother asked, throwing up her hands in frustration.

On many occasions, afterward I recalled my mother's words. In my career as a teacher and rebbetzin, I would be consulted by parents and children.

I would first turn to the teenager. "Tell me what the problem is."

"*I* have no problems," would be the quick retort. "*She* has the problem," the girl would say, pointing to her mother with disdain.

"Who is 'she'?" I would ask patiently.

And sometimes it would take as much as ten minutes before the child could pronounce the simple word "mother."

As I observed the impudence of teenagers and the virtuous anger with which they related to their elders, I became more and more aware of the terrible toll that the abandonment of religion has taken on our twentieth-century culture.

In our society, young people are cast into adulthood rather than allowed to mature into it. Their conditioning process starts early: Their toys, their mannerisms, their values, are all part of the conspiracy. For example, instead of the traditional dolls that require cuddling and loving care, little girls are given sophisticated models that, with their chic hairdos and magnificent wardrobes, exemplify the ultimate in conspicuous consumption.

The fashion scene is even more corrupt, for children are encouraged not only to emulate mom and dad in their dress, but to wear sexually provocative attire and ape suggestive adult behavior. By the time they reach the sixth grade, not only have they attended dances and dated, but most likely they have even had some sexual experience. Thus thrown into the adult world without being prepared for it, they remain permanently immature, confused, and unstable.

In every culture, the transition from childhood to adulthood can be agonizingly painful, but in our society this passage is even more turbulent, for it is made without adequate structure or traditional guidelines. If maturity is to be achieved, the family must first provide the necessary support and direction. Our entire religion is based on this concept: the transmittance of a heritage from generation to generation, the eternal link that binds father to son, mother to daughter.

If authentic Judaism has had difficulty taking root in America, it is partially due to the erosion of the family. It is difficult to relate to a Heavenly Father without first having established a relationship with an earthly parent. It is through our ancestors that we, the Jewish people, have learned to communicate with our G-d. It is their names that we invoke as we rise thrice daily in prayer for silent meditation, and it is by the names of our parents that we are identified when we are called up to the Holy Torah. But alas, today's generation does not know its own Jewish names, let alone those of its fathers.

It is written that when King Solomon erected the Temple in Jerusalem, he attempted to bring the Holy Ark into the Sanctuary, but the gates locked and would not open for him.

King Solomon began to pray, and chanted hymns in praise of G-d, but the gates remained closed. Then Solomon raised his voice and commanded: "Open, ye gates, allow the L-rd of Hosts to enter!" But still, the gates remained locked.

In desperation, Solomon cried out: "Almighty G-d, remember the righteousness of David, my father!" Instantly, the gates opened and the Holy Ark was brought into the Sanctuary.

There are moments in every man's existence when life's gates lock against him, when he feels trapped and hopeless. If at such times he could only echo the words of Solomon, his forefathers would come forth, show him the way, and lead him to those still waters for which his soul so desperately yearns. But alienated from his father, cut off from his past, contemporary man does not know how to recall the righteousness of his ancestors. Yet, if he is to make it, he has no recourse but to find his way back, for only through that timeless path will he be able to discover his Creator and live.

It is this path that I uncovered one winter morning in the home of my grandparents in Nadudvar. The times that I spent with them were among the happiest memories of my childhood. I can still see them standing in front of their great big rambling house, awaiting our arrival. As our horse-drawn carriage pulled up, they joyously rushed toward us and clasped us in their arms. While we stood there, enveloped in their love, we were convinced that we were the luckiest children alive.

"My *teire kinderlach*, my precious little ones," my grandmother would say, fussing over us as she led us into the house. "What would you like to eat? I have everything prepared just for you!"

Eagerly, we would follow her into the enormous kitchen, our mouths watering in anticipation of the many delicacies that we knew awaited us. In my grandparents' home, every meal was a party, and every day an adventure in wonderland.

In retrospect, it seems odd that we children experienced so much excitement there, for to be quite candid, there wasn't much to keep us amused, but my grandparents always found some marvelous ways to ignite our imagination. There was a special treasure chest that my grandmother kept just for us, her "precious little ones." It was a great box filled with all manner of fascinating things: buttons of various shapes and colors, bits of ribbon and lace, trinkets of no special value or significance, but to us they were wondrous, and far more exciting than the expensive toys found in today's nurseries.

What I recall most vividly from those early childhood

days were the times when my grandfather would allow me to accompany him to his study. I adored these visits to his library. I loved to sit at his feet, playing my silent games to the rhythmic sound of his sweet voice chanting passages from the Holy Books. And how very special I felt, when for a moment he would interrupt his studies, pour himself some hot tea, and beckon me to bring the plate with the little cubes of sugar.

"Thank you, my precious little one," he would smile, as he took the sugar and lifted me to his knee. "It's time for you and me to have some refreshment."

How can I convey the joy that I felt as I bit into those delicious cubes and sipped the hot golden liquid? How can I relate those marvelous stories that my grandfather would tell, and how can I communicate the security and contentment that I experienced as he held me in his arms and I fell asleep, his long white beard covering my head?

My grandfather was a saintly man, a rabbi, a sage. His beautiful face always radiated kindness and inner peace. I never saw him lose his temper, display anger, or even become annoyed. He was a man of G-d, and his very presence communicated serenity, warmth, and holiness.

One cold winter morning, I ventured alone into my *zeide*'s study. I looked forward to sitting on his knee and sharing some tea with him again, but when I opened the door, I became terribly frightened. My *zeide* was sitting in his chair, the huge books opened before him, but instead of singing the melody with which he usually studied Torah, my *zeide* was crying.

In a panic, I ran to my father. "*Tatie! Tatie!* Something horrible must have happened. *Zeide* is crying!"

My father took me by the hand. "Come, my child," he said reassuringly, "let's take a walk outside and I will explain it all to you."

As my father dressed me in my winter coat and boots, I

noticed that his eyes were also moist with tears. Slowly, we began to walk, but because the snow was very deep, my father instructed me to walk behind him and follow in his footsteps. We had only gone a short way, when my father paused and pointed to the path we had made in the fresh, clean snow. Bending down to me, he asked gently, "Do you know why I walked ahead of you?"

"Yes," I replied readily, "so that I wouldn't fall, so that I could follow in your footsteps."

My father nodded, his eyes expressing satisfaction with my answer. "But it is not only in deep snow that a parent must make a path for his children. There is another road, a road that you, my child, do not understand as yet. It is a road that is fraught with hardship, a road upon which many embark only to fall. It is that road which your *zeide* is preparing for us with his tears. When your *zeide* studies the Holy Books, he not only studies to acquire knowledge for himself, but he studies in order to make the way for us, his children. He utters a prayer and sheds a tear so that we may all be learned of the Torah, followers of G-d's Commandments, and thus claim our heritage."

I was only a litttle girl of five at the time. I did not fully understand the import of my father's words, but the memory of my *zeide*'s tears never left me, and in difficult moments I would hear my father's voice whispering, prodding me on: "It's easy. Your *zeide* made the way for us. You have only to follow in his footsteps."

It all happened many years ago, before Hitler's henchmen gutted my grandparents' beautiful home, before my beloved *zeide* and *bubba*, together with my many little cousins, were deported to Auschwitz and cast into the flames. A lone survivor related to us that my *zeide* refused to abandon his little grandchildren, and with his last breath tried to shield them from the poisonous gasses. And I am certain that as he did so, his tears continued to fall, and he thought of us, his precious little ones, and paved the way for yet another generation.

With the passage of time, the Almighty, in His infinite mercy, granted me the privilege of giving life to my first son, and in the midst of my joy I remembered those tears. I named my son "Yisroel," in memory of my *zeide*, and I prayed that he, together with all my children, might continue to walk that well-trodden path, that he might follow in the footsteps and become yet another link in that glorious heritage.

Years later, when my son became Bar Mitzvaed, my dear father quoted to him the Biblical passage assigned for that Sabbath: "Now then, Yisroel, what doth the L-rd your G-d require of thee? Only that you revere the L-rd your G-d, that you walk in His path" (*Deuteronomy* 11:12).

"Is reverence of G-d such a simple matter," my father asked, "that the Bible should minimize it by using the diminutive only'?"

And even as he posed the question, he answered by saying: "Yes, it is a simple matter for you my child, for you had a grandfather who paved the way. You need only follow in his footsteps."

My father's name is Abraham, and as he spoke I could have sworn that I heard the voice of the first Abraham. My grandfathers, my ancestors, were fused into one. I looked at my son and I was overcome by an indescribable feeling of joy. I wanted to shout and proclaim: "Listen, world! My *Zeide* Yisroel, who was cast into the flames of the crematorium, never perished. My son is walking in his footsteps!"

Every one of us in his past had a grandfather who paved the way with tears of love. That road is waiting to be discovered, to lead us back to our roots, to our heritage.

But how? How do you uncover that timeless path? How do you draw from that fount of wisdom? How do you actually go about opening those ancient gates of the fathers?

Roy Neuberger, Jr. (who today is our *Hineni* hospitality chairman), was in 1974 the editor of an upstate New York newspaper. He was writing a story on the phenomenon of Jewish revival. When he came to interview me, he presented me with this very challenge.

I invited Roy to open the Holy Books, and as he studied, he discovered that he, Roy, an American, was part of the greatest drama to unfold in the annals of history. His ancestors had sealed a Covenant with G-d, and with Bible in hand, went forth to the four corners of the world to become a blessing unto all mankind. But this dispersion was just a prelude to a greater destiny that would see his people return to the land to become a light unto the nations and usher in peace for all humanity.

For the first time, Roy understood the meaning of his people's suffering, for that, too, had been foretold in G-d's Book. And with that, he also gained an insight into his own frustrations: "Because they shall forsake Me and break My Covenant which I have made with them, they shall be devoured by many evils" (*Deuteronomy* 28:15).

It all became clear to him. Divorced from G-d, he could never hope to survive. With his newfound insight, Roy attached himself with fervor to his heritage. Henceforth, his life and the life of his family would be fused with the timeless past. The Book demanded that he elevate his every thought, his every act, into a Divine service. "Ye shall be holy unto Me, for I, the L-rd your G-d, am holy" (*Leviticus* 19:2).

Roy read the words over and over again. They penetrated to the depths of his soul, and a total transformation took place in his life. His most instinctive acts and mechanical reactions came under G-d's purview. "I feel as if all my life I had been toying with a jigsaw puzzle, and suddenly, the pieces fit," he confided.

But of all the changes that Roy underwent, the discovery

of the Sabbath had the greatest impact on him. Roy, like his contemporaries, was caught on an endless merry-go-round. He lived by the clock and was always on the go. Even when he was determined to relax, he felt a compulsion to work. As a matter of fact, there were times when he exerted more effort having fun than in putting in a full day at the office. But then he discovered the Sabbath, and a new calm descended on him. From the moment that his wife kindled the Sabbath lights, he was able to make contact with his inner self and reach out to his wife and children in a way that he was never able to do before. With the advent of the Sabbath, Roy was actually able to divorce himself from his environment and enter a world that was separate in time. The phone could ring, but he would feel no compulsion to answer it. The mail arrived, and it remained unopened, the T.V., the radio, the hi-fi, were all silenced. Roy discovered a new sense of freedom. It was as if G-d Himself came to relieve his burdens, to soothe his brow, and calm his nerves. The day had a power of its own which could not be simulated at any other time, for the Almighty Himself rested on the Seventh Day and He Himself blessed it. To desist from work on that day was to join the Creator in partnership and to partake of the blessing of peace that He granted.

By observing the Sabbath, Roy unlocked those ancient gates of his fathers. Every aspect of the day was a reminder of his past, a link with his roots: The two loaves of challah on the table recalled the manna that sustained his people while they traversed the Sinai desert; the snowy white cloth brought to mind the layers of dew in which G-d enveloped the Heavenly bread; the wine was a cup of sanctification with which his grandfathers glorified G-d's Day of Rest; and the two candlesticks were reminders of the double Commandment to observe and hallow the Sabbath. In the glow of the candlelight, Roy gathered his children and bestowed upon them the blessings with which the patriarch Jacob blessed his own children: "May G-d make thee like Ephraim and Menashe . . . May G-d make thee like Sarah, Rebecca, Rachel, and Leah . . . May the L-rd bless thee and keep thee. May He cause His Countenance to shine upon thee and be gracious unto thee. May the L-rd turn His Countenance unto thee and grant thee peace."

As his hands rested upon his children's heads, the petty angers that had divided his family during the week evaporated. Angels and patriarchs entered his home and renewed his soul. The Sabbath had come. The gates had unlocked, and Roy had only to follow in the footsteps.

I write so that the gates may unlock for all of us, so that we may all uncover that ancient path, but if we are to do so, we will first have to understand why and how we lost it.

three

THE AMERICAN
JEWISH EXPERIENCE

BACK IN THE LATE sixties, when student rebellion was at its peak, I was invited to speak at a New York City high school. The school had instituted a very successful Afro-Asian studies program, and as a result, some members of the faculty were anxious to introduce a parallel program of Jewish studies.

A few days prior to my scheduled appearance, a department head called to advise me that there had been some rioting, and it might be best to postpone my talk. But the program had been publicized, and I, for one, was not planning to back down.

When I arrived at the school, I found tensions running high, and decided to try to cool the atmosphere by throwing out some questions.

"Tell me," I asked as an opener, "if G-d wished to populate the world, why did He create only one couple, Adam and Eve?"

The students, not accustomed to religious discussion or Biblical references, did not quite know what to make of my question.

"G-d specifically wished for us to have one common ancestor," I went on to explain, "so that none of us—black, white, or yellow, might claim descent from a superior race.

We are all the children of the same Heavenly Father and the same earthly parents. We are all brothers and sisters, and in the end, that's the only thing that counts. So what do you say, let's stop all this bickering."

I searched for some Jewish faces in the crowd. Before speaking on Jewish studies, I thought it might be a good idea to have one of the students comment on the subject, but the eyes that met mine were cold and indifferent.

"Is there someone here who can discuss Judaism?" I asked. "Surely there must be someone who has knowledge of the Bible or the prophets. After all, we are the People of the Book. Who should be familiar with it if not us?"

But none of the students were willing to take up my challenge.

"It's not that we don't want to speak or that we're ashamed of being Jewish," one of the boys finally volunteered. "I went to Hebrew school and was Bar Mitzvaed, but I never learned a damn thing, and to tell the truth, I don't know anyone who did."

It was a bitter pill for me to swallow, and it occurred to me that the extermination of our people was still going on, but with one fine difference: In the crematoria, our bodies were consumed, while here our souls were being snuffed out. In a way, I found this second death more painful to accept, for those who perished in the gas chambers had no options, but these young people were orchestrating their own deaths. In the concentration camps, with our last breaths we reaffirmed our faith, but these boys and girls had no faith to affirm. To have survived thousands of years, to have endured exile, torture, and death, only to vanish in the free world, was a nightmare to which I could not reconcile myself.

As I looked at the students, I recalled a funeral at which my husband had officiated. It was one of those situations in which the chapel called because the family did not have its own rabbi. An old lady had died and she was survived by three sons. All three had intermarried, and the grandchildren were no longer Jewish.

With the demise of the old lady, a history of thousands of years had come to an end. A branch had died on a tree, a family had disappeared. Strange, I thought to myself, that these kids who could stand on street corners collecting signatures for the preservation of endangered species never realized that it was *they* who had become an endangered species.

I was overcome by a terrible sadness. How many of these students, I wondered, would survive as Jews, and how many would disappear in assimilation. Then it occurred to me that most of them probably didn't even understand that they were missing something, that they had been Jewishly shortchanged. Perhaps, I thought, by listening to a parable, they might gain a glimmer of their deprivation.

"Long, long ago," I began, "we had an ancestor who was renowned for his saintliness. Every day he would go to a forest, and there kindle a mystical fire, chant prayers, and serve G-d.

"When he died, his descendents continued his tradition. They, too, went to the forest and kindled the sacred fire, but alas, they had forgotten the prayer. Nevertheless, in their own way, they continued to worship G-d.

"The next generation, however, not only forgot the prayer, but they also lost the mystical wisdom through which to kindle the fire. Still, they would gather in the forest and recall the sanctity of their father, and through that recollection, they managed to find their way to G-d.

"Then came a generation that could no longer remember, a generation without a past—*our generation*."

I looked straight at the students now. "Our ancestors were prophets and sages," I said, "and today we are not even capable of explaining a simple Biblical passage. If you would only think about it, you too would feel the enormity of our loss."

Then a girl raised her hand. "Why didn't our parents teach us? Why did they allow us to lose our heritage?" she asked.

The question was simple enough, but the answer, I'm afraid, would not be so easily forthcoming.

I invited the students to consider the typical grandpa and determine how he, with his love for Judaism, could have compromised his beliefs and traditions and condoned the superficial sham which went under the guise of Jewish education for his children.

Perhaps, I suggested, through Tevye, the legendary character from Sholom Aleichem's *Fiddler On The Roof*, we can understand, for sometimes a fictitious figure is the best mirror of our actual predicament.

Tevye was a simple man, endowed with great faith, but alas, little education. He dreamt of the day when he would become rich and spend all his time studying G-d's Holy Word, and if, in the interim, his Biblical references and quotes were inaccurate, he was confident that the Almighty, his best friend, would understand and forgive.

Despite all his plans, Tevye never became rich, nor did he become a Torah scholar, but he did get to the United States, the land of golden opportunity, where, if a man was willing to work hard, there was no telling how far he could go. No task was too difficult for Tevye, no job beneath him. Willingly, he slaved in the sweatshops, lived in a tenement, and pushed a pushcart in the hope that one day his son, if not he, would make it.

Tevye became Americanized, changed his name to Morris, and set new goals for himself and his children. Instead of encouraging his son to become a rabbi, Tevye

pressured him to become a professional, for he quickly realized that in the United States, education was the gateway to
economic opportunity, and under such circumstances, it
would be sheer madness to let his son waste time poring over
ancient tomes. It is not that Grandpa Morris loved his Judaism any less than before, but to him, Torah study was associated with the poverty of the *shtetl*, and he couldn't bear to
consign his son to that.

To be sure, there were some fears that life in America
presented to him (not the least being that his son Miltie
might marry out of the faith), but Morris took a strong stand
and warned his son that he would sit *shiva* (consider him
dead) before he would ever accept such a union. With that,
he was content that he had adequately prepared his child for
Jewish life.

Miltie's Jewish education was not only shallow, but
worse, it terminated at the age of thirteen, before it ever had
a chance to get started. Any interest that Miltie may have
had in his studies was thwarted by his Hebrew teachers,
whose stock answer to all his questions was, "Don't ask,
that's how it's gotta be!" Nor did Miltie fare any better at
home. Turned off by the double standard of his family (at
home it's kosher, outside you look away), he found religious
life a hypocritical farce.

As Miltie advanced in his secular studies, he found himself becoming more and more alienated from the faith of his
ancestors. In time, he became the successful doctor that his
father had hoped he would be, but something went sour
along the way. There was an ever-growing gap between
father and son. Miltie was embarrassed by the old man's
manner, his accent, his boorishness. He was determined to
free himself from the shackles of the ghetto, to climb the
social ladder, and to raise his child without Jewish guilt. He
and his wife, Shirley, moved to a suburban community

where people were more American than Jewish, where there were no reminders of their ancient past.

Miltie did not want his son to undergo the harrowing experiences that he had to contend with in his own youth, and so, when the time came to register Kevin for Bar Mitzva lessons, Miltie made it quite clear that Kevin was not to be subjected to any religious pressure. Whether he would go to synagogue on Sabbath morning or to little league would be his decision alone to make.

Kevin's Hebrew education was no improvement over his father's—the meaningless repetition of the *Haftorah* (a passage from the prophets recited on the day of Bar Mitzva), memorization of prayers which he did not understand, and stories that bored him to tears. And yet, there were some differences. Instead of laying down the law, declaring, "That's how it's gotta be," Kevin's rabbis bent over backward to be sympathetic, but in the process they also snuffed out any religious fire which may have burned in his soul. At least the old-time rabbis were able to communicate some zeal; at least Grandpa Morris, who felt passionate about his faith, was able to evoke a sense of Jewish guilt in Miltie, but Kevin was deprived even of that. His father was indifferent to his Jewishness, and his teachers could not reach him. Kevin was a spiritual orphan.

The Bar Mitzva party was the focal point of Kevin's Jewishness. Shirley and Miltie spared no effort to make it a success. Miltie recalled that Morris couldn't afford to make anything elaborate when he was Bar Mitzvaed, so in a way, Kevin's celebration was going to be his party as well.

At synagogue, Miltie could hardly wait for the prayers to be over. He had difficulty following the Hebrew, and was worried about the reaction of his gentile guests. Fortunately, the services concluded without incident. Everyone was satisfied that, indeed, Kevin had outdone himself. But were you to have asked Kevin what it meant to be a Jew, were you to have asked him about the Five Books of Moses, the Mishna, the Talmud, the Prophets, he could not have answered, and yet his Jewish education was over.

The high school years proved to be traumatic for Kevin. He became moody and insolent. He drank and experimented with drugs and sex. Miltie and Shirley tried to console themselves by attributing his problems to the complexity of society and the many pressures that young people have to contend with nowadays. They kept hoping that Kevin's rebelliousness was just a stage, that in time, he would get hold of himself and straighten out.

Miltie tried to reach his son, but nothing seemed to work. He bought tickets to ballgames, played tennis, and regularly took Kevin out to dinner, but it was all to no avail. As a matter of fact, at times Miltie had an uncanny suspicion that the more he tried to relate to Kevin, the greater the contempt he evoked. On occasion, when Miltie caught Kevin's eye, he had the feeling that the boy was embarrassed by him. How ironic that Miltie, who had suffered so from his father's boorishness, should now suspect that his own son was equally uncomfortable with him.

Kevin lived in a beautiful home, but he felt hemmed in.

Kevin had been given everything that money could buy, but he felt deprived.

Kevin had understanding parents who were willing to accept him on his own terms, yet Kevin felt abandoned and alone.

Kevin could communicate with strangers, but there was a wall between himself and his parents.

Kevin could sympathize with every oppressed people, but he had difficulty relating to his own.

Kevin went off to college, but no sooner did he begin his studies than he decided to drop out.

"I have to find myself," he explained to his bewildered parents. "I'm not sure about my goals. I need time to think, to travel, to get my head together."

Alienated from G-d and lacking the structure of religion, Kevin was spiritually adrift. He attempted to satisfy his quest by gravitating from drugs to Christian communes, from Hindu ashrams to meditation centers, but it was all to no avail. He could not find peace.

Shirley and Miltie reached their middle years. They, too, became disillusioned. Things did not turn out as they had hoped. But it wasn't only Kevin who disappointed them. Their marriage had also fallen apart. Their heightened affluence not only failed to bring them happiness, but worse, it accentuated the superficiality of their lifestyle. The more they indulged their obsession with pleasure, the greater their frustration became. Overcome by a sense of despair, they spent a fortune on analysis and self-discovery programs, but to no end. They lacked beliefs to latch onto, values to sustain them, and their marriage collapsed.

Grandpa Morris retired to Miami. He could not understand where he had gone wrong. The whole thing was beyond him. "When Miltie was a boy," he mused, "I worried that he become an American, and today I'm worried that Kevin, my grandson, remain a Jew. It's a strange world."

The American Jewish experience has come full cycle. Grandpa Morris bartered Torah education for a university degree, and he succeeded so well that today he lives in fear of losing his grandchildren.

Kevin, the heir to the "good life," is spiritually homeless. Not only is he the victim of Jewish illiteracy, but of the crisis in Western civilization as well. The rapidly changing mores, the breakdown of the traditional family, the anonymity of the computer society, have all contributed to his spiritual angst. If only he knew the Bible, he would very likely cry out: "Not by bread alone does man live!" (*Deuteronomy*

8:3). But even that consolation is denied him. His ignorance of Judaism precludes him from identifying his personal quest with the greater yearning of his people. And so, Kevin resorts to the only method available to him and attempts to express his feelings through a letter:

Dear Mom and Dad:

At the outset, let me assure you that I am grateful for all the things that you have given me. No, I'm not being sarcastic. I really do feel appreciative, but please understand, I need something more, and I know that I must find it.

Now, please don't try to analyze me, and don't try to attribute my problems to emotional instability, insecurity, and all that jazz. For once in your life, treat me as a human being and not like a case.

Do you remember how you were always pressuring me about school and marks? Then, one day, I asked why my grades were so important, and you said, "Kevin, you must go to college, you must have an education." Was it really for an education that you wanted me to go to college, or was it to assure that I make it big?

Don't get me wrong. I'm not against earning money, but for me there must be something more to life than making a buck. So I left college, not because I was confused (as you tried to imply), but because before I became a workhorse, I wanted to know what I was working for. I was determined to devote my life to something meaningful. But that you did not want to understand.

Remember, Mom, the time I joined an ashram and how you carried on about the fine Jewish education I betrayed? At first, I couldn't believe that you actually said that. What Jewish education were you talking about? Those Bar Mitzva lessons? Or perhaps you were referring to the Junior Congregation that I had to attend while you and Dad went off to the club to play tennis.

You know as well as I that I never had a Jewish education to speak of, and there was never a semblance of religion in our home. Let's face it, it wasn't the fact that I joined another religion that got to you. What really cut you up was that I didn't turn out to be the success that you dreamt of, that you couldn't parade me in front of your friends. Your son, the college student with a brilliant future, became a bum, and that you couldn't handle.

Dad, you kept badgering me about making a living, reminding me every minute that at my age you had to hold down two jobs and help support the family while working your way through college. Well, I'm really sorry that you had to go through all that, but I don't see why I have to be constantly reminded of it. Although you may think you gave me everything, I also had my struggles. I felt lost and frustrated; I searched for purpose, values, a sense of pride in living, but you never showed me where to find it. I'm not blaming you, but instead of pushing me to the psychiatrist, I wish you would try to understand.

KEVIN

Like Kevin, the average contemporary Jewish youth has no knowledge of his heritage, nor does he have Jewish memories to sustain him. To be sure, the previous generation did not fare much better educationally, but nevertheless they were buttressed by a colorful panorama of Jewish experiences. The very streets on which Miltie and his peers grew up teemed with Jewishness. There were kosher markets, *shuls* on every corner, men with long black coats and beards. On Fridays, in anticipation of the Sabbath, there was always a sense of excitement in the air punctuated by scintillating aromas of fresh-baked challah, kugel, and gefilte fish. Above all, there were Yiddish-speaking *bubbas* and *zeides* with whom the children were able to spend the Sabbath and holidays.

Now, while such emotional underpinnings were not a replacement for genuine scholarship or knowledge, they did foster a Jewish consciousness, which, if nothing else, prevented defection and conversion.

Kevin, on the other hand, had no such Jewish memories to anchor him. In contrast to his father, Miltie, who wanted to run away from his religion, Kevin never had a religion to run away from. Sabbath to him was Saturday, a day for shopping or little league, and *bubba* and *zeide* were "grandma" and "grandpa," living in a remote retirement village. Raised in a Jewish vacuum, Kevin was the victim of an educational system that had collapsed, of a family that had disintegrated, and of a nation that had assimilated. In his psychology-oriented environment, there were no absolutes to guide him—everything was negotiable.

His parents prided themselves on being open and understanding, and were prepared to accept his experiments with sex and his dabbling in drugs and alcohol. Instead of appreciating this parental tolerance, Kevin interpreted it as lack of concern, and therefore did not feel the same obligation to give *naches*, joy, to his parents that Miltie had. Self-righteously, he asserted that everything was coming to him, and the more he was indulged, the more meaningless it all became.

By the time he reached the age of eighteen, Kevin had tried every scene, but he remained restless and dissatisfied. In his quest for meaning, he was prepared to undertake any challenge—nothing fazed him; the more ascetic the group, the greater its attraction, and his thirst was such that even the bizarre became mystical in his eyes. He was ready to try anything except his own religion, which he was convinced had nothing more to offer than the Bar Mitzva lessons which he had already experienced.

Kevin and his generation are suffering, not from a want of things, but from a lack of spirituality, a yearning that the prophet Amos foresaw: "And days shall come upon you, saith the L-rd, and I shall send a hunger into the land. Not a hunger for bread, nor a thirst for water, but a hunger for the Word of G-d" (*Amos* 9:11).

If this hunger is to be satiated, if Kevin and his generation are to find fulfillment, they will not only have to immerse themselves in Judaism, but they will have to liberate themselves from the inhibiting chains of our cultural value system, for not only do they suffer from Jewish neglect, but from the corrosive influence of Western culture as well. They belong to the generation that has learned to walk on the moon while it has lost its way here on earth, the generation that has laid its stakes in the shifting sands of the twentieth century rather than in the timeless values of G-d's Torah.

We have come full cycle—from Tevye to Morris, to Miltie to Kevin.

My story ended, and as I looked at the students, their eyes told me that they understood, for they each had something of Kevin in them.

"So, where do we go from here?" a boy called out.

"Now the ball is in your court," I answered. "Only you will be able to decide who will be the son of Kevin. Only you will be able to determine whether he will rediscover his Jewish name, or disappear as the old lady's grandchildren had."

Yes, Kevin has become an endangered species, and if he is to make it, we will have to reconstruct for him that traditional family life which enabled our people to survive the centuries.

🌰

four

BEGINNINGS OF FAMILY LIFE

How to Build a Family –
How to Find a Mate

DESPITE THE FACT THAT most of our relatives had been wiped
out during the Holocaust, I grew up feeling I had a very
large family. Every day, I acquired new "cousins," "aunts,"
and "uncles," who, through the warmth and love of my parents, were made to feel that they were a part of us.

Whenever I came home from school, they were there:
newly arrived immigrants seeking my father's counsel, lonely
souls who had been invited for dinner, or friends who had
just dropped in to say hello. My parents referred to them all
as *mishpocha*, family.

In order for me to get from my home in East Flatbush to
a *yeshiva*, parochial school, located in Williamsburg, I had
to travel by two buses, and always during rush hour. This
meant that I hardly ever got a seat, and worse, I was the sort
of kid who quickly became carsick. No sooner did I inhale
the gasoline fumes than I would dash for the exit, and at the
nearest curb begin to retch. Often I arrived at school late,
green, and exhausted.

The hours were long, from 8:30 in the morning until 6:00
at night, and I faced the same miserable bus ride on the way
home. But after such a grueling day, it never occurred to me
that I should resent the strangers sitting around our kitchen
table, or that I should want to have my mother all to myself.

Nor did I feel I needed privacy, time to unwind in tranquil surroundings. Only years later, did I discover that in America homes were meant to be private places, that visitors could come only by appointment, that meals were supposed to be prepared in amounts sufficient for family members, and that pots could actually become empty (my mother's always seemed bottomless).

When dinner was over, we would do our homework at the table while my mother turned to her mending. We always studied to the accompaniment of my mother's quiet humming and the quick, rhythmic motion of her hands. There was very little help that my mother could lend us. To the newly arrived immigrant, English, and the American school curriculum, were, at best, a mystery. But as I struggled with my math problems, my mother's presence seemed to make things easier. Her sympathetic sigh told me that she understood how difficult all this was, and that, to me, was the greatest source of encouragement.

Again, I never thought that in order to do my homework efficiently, I was entitled to my own room, my own desk, and undisturbed quiet. Nor did it ever enter my mind that because of my foreign background I had the right to feel disadvantaged, that I could cop out by using my harrowing experiences in the concentration camps to justify poor school performance, or that I could blame my parents and teachers for my problems. My responsibilities were always clearly delineated: To live my life in such a way that I might bring *naches,* joy, to my parents, and honor to my G-d. To have failed in this area would have been tantamount to betrayal, for which I could blame no one but myself.

Rationalizations like, "I didn't ask to be born," and "My parents owe it to me," were simply foreign to my experience. In my world, it was the children who owed everything to their parents, and although our obligations were never articulated, we nevertheless realized that no matter what we did, we could never totally fulfill our indebtedness. I guess that it was partially because of this feeling that I found it so hard to accept the nonchalance with which my newfound American friends related to their parents.

I particularly remember Gloria, who lived on our block. She was going steady with a non-Jewish boy (which to me in itself was shocking), but what I found even more incredible was that she appeared to be completely indifferent to the feelings of her parents. Despite the fact that her father suffered a coronary and her mother cried incessantly, Gloria merely shrugged her shoulders. "I'm sorry," she said matter of factly, "but I have to think about my own happiness."

How could she hope to find happiness, I wondered, knowing that her parents were heartsick? How could she sleep at night, knowing that she was the cause of her mother's tears?

Many years have since passed, and I have yet to understand how any individual can hope to build a life, knowing that he is the cause of the suffering of his dear ones. Surely there is something desperately wrong with our way of relating to the members of our family if we can be so indifferent to their feelings, if we fail to comprehend that family life is based on mutual concern and interdependence. Despite all the clever slogans that assure us that what we do is strictly our own business, we cannot divorce ourselves from the needs of our families without paying a severe penalty.

A woman who had run off with her boyfriend and abandoned her children confided to me that while she was fine during the day, she would awaken in the middle of the night with the most horrible feeling in the pit of her stomach. She twisted and turned, and could fall back to sleep again only with the help of pills.

"I was able to close the door on my family," she said pathetically, "but I could not shut them out."

To have a family is to understand that your life is not

your own, that you have a responsibility to those who are near and dear to you. Judaism recognizes this truth, and therefore enjoins us to become involved in the lives of our children, even if they should regard such involvement as meddling.

In contrast, contemporary culture assures us that we can best demonstrate our love for our children by respecting their independence, by keeping our distance, and by allowing them to work things out for themselves. We forget, however, that there is a world of difference between *living someone's life for him or her,* and *being supportive,* between *dictating* and *guiding.* Undoubtedly, striking a proper balance is not always easy, but that is what parenting is all about. To have children is the greatest of all responsibilities, a sacred trust which must be invested with spiritual and moral dimensions. Therefore, in our family, it never occurred to any of us to question the prerogative of our parents or elders to guide and direct us.

I had a great-aunt whom we all called "Tante." As the senior member of the family, she had the undisputed right to involve herself in our lives. Tante was a tall, handsome woman, with a quick wit, a ready sense of humor, and a sharp, peppery tongue, which everyone loved and feared. She was an expert in every field. If one of us fell ill, it was Tante who told the doctor what *really* was wrong. She had her own nostrums for every disease, and relatives as well as friends were always consulting her.

Tante was an original. Today she would probably be called an ecologist. Out of sheer necessity and dire financial need, she learned how to create everything from basic natural ingredients. From cooking to canning, from the latest in haute couture clothing to do-it-yourself dry cleaning, Tante was master of all. But more important, she was always available and willing to share her talents with us. It was Tante who made my graduation dress, and it was she who directed the cooking and baking for every family gathering. Tante was infallible. She had her finger in every pie, and she never hesitated to express her opinions.

On *Shabbos* afternoon, our family would always gather. Tante would usually come to us, but if for some reason she couldn't make it, we eagerly made the long trek to her house. In addition to the myriad stories with which she would entertain us, Tante always set a table laden with the finest delicacies. But it wasn't only her marvelous tales and incredible pastries that drew us. Even more magnetic were the family deliberations over which she presided which made every Saturday afternoon an adventure in the court of human relations. At these gatherings, everything and anything was discussed, from our school studies and social life to our plans for the future. Admittedly, there were times when we resented these intrusions on our privacy, but the knowledge that we were not alone, that the entire family stood behind us and was ready to go to bat for our every need, overrode all other considerations.

We never experienced the malaise of loneliness and alienation which plagues so many young people nowadays. Despite the many traumas of our childhood, my brothers and I never felt abandoned or frightened, and it was all due to a strong and loving family. I must also add that this loving concern was not limited to the children, but was extended to all who passed our way.

FINDING A PROPER MATE

I remember when our cousin Sheindel came to the United States only a few months after our own arrival. Sheindel was a cousin thrice removed, but from the way my parents took her into our home, she could have been my sister. Her family had been killed in Auschwitz, and my mother and father naturally assumed the obligation of caring for her. No sooner had Sheindel settled in, than one *Shabbos* afternoon Tante announced that since she had reached the ripe old age of twenty, it was time to find her a proper *shidduch*—husband.

Now, most people would interpret a *shidduch* as a pre-arranged match in which two people are forced into matrimony. But that is totally misleading. A *shidduch* simply means that the boy or girl whom you will date comes highly recommended by a mutual acquaintance who acts as the *shadchan*, recommender. Traditional Jewish families have always preferred to have their children meet their mates through reliable introductions rather than through pick-ups or casual meetings. Marriage was simply too important to be left to chance. Therefore, when Tante counseled Sheindel in her choice of a mate, it was not out of a desire to control or manipulate, but rather out of genuine concern for her future. Marriage was probably the most decisive and far-reaching decision that Sheindel would ever have to make, and because of this, Tante felt a responsibility to share her own experience and the cumulative wisdom of our ancestors.

"In every marriage, you have to give a little and take a little, but when it comes to *character* and *breeding*," Tante warned, "you just can't afford to compromise, because that's one thing that if a boy doesn't have, he will never acquire. The way he saw his father behave toward his mother, that's how he will behave toward you one day. Remember, Sheindel, it's not what school he went to, but what he saw at home that counts, and if he doesn't come from a refined family, no amount of education will make him a gentleman.

"So, my dear, don't get carried away by the superficial things which dazzle girls nowadays: the profession, the money, the car. Judge a boy by what he *is* rather than by what he *does*, for ultimately, the only thing that counts is that he be well-versed in the Torah, that he come from a good family, and that he be a *mensch.*"

Now *mensch* is a Yiddish word which is difficult to translate. Its literal meaning is "to be a man." But it is much more than that. It encompasses compassion and common sense, a wisdom which transcends book learning. In short, a *mensch* says and does the right thing at the right time.

"Make sure that the boy you go out with is a *mensch*, that you have common goals," Tante warned, "because you will never change him. As he is, so he will remain."

And just in case Sheindel had missed the point, Tante reminded her of Minna, a sweet but dizzy girl who became the laughingstock of the neighborhood when she splurged on a very expensive pair of shoes that she was never able to wear.

"To tell the truth," Tante would tell us, "the shoes were really beautiful, but when she told me that they weren't her size, I couldn't believe my ears. 'Minna,' I said, 'how could you be such a fool, to spend so much money on shoes that don't fit?'

"Minna became annoyed and insisted that the salesman had assured her that in time the shoes would give and be comfortable. In vain did I warn her," Tante said, "that shoes that don't fit when you buy them will never be any good. Minna refused to listen, and walked around like a cripple. She had the shoes stretched and threw good money after bad, but of course, nothing helped, the shoes never fit."

And now Tante, who had a flair for the dramatic, paused and solemnly declared: "Finding the right man is no different from finding the right shoes. *If they are not your size, they can never be made to fit!* In the store, it's easy to disregard that 'little' pinch, that 'little' irritation, but the aches and pains that start when you return home cannot be so readily ignored. On a date, it's easy to overlook shortcomings but when you get home and you have to share a life together, then it's a different story. That's when the truth comes out. So, Sheindel, don't forget, if the shoes are not your size, if the boy is not your type, you can be crippled for the rest of your life."

And to reinforce her words, Tante clued Sheindel into our sages' prescription for uncovering a boy's character: "It can all be summed up through the 'Three K's of the Talmud,' " Tante would say, b'*Kisso*, b'*Kasso*, b'*Kosso*: his *pocket*, his *temper*, his *cups*, meaning, is he stingy, hard, or selfish? Is he ill-humored, hot-tempered? Is he given to shouting and cursing? Does he make painful jibes at the expense of others? Is he considerate? Does he have manners? Is he respectful of his elders, or is he a glutton who sees only his own needs? Be on the lookout, Sheindel, for these 'little things.' In the long run, that's all that really matters, for even the most handsome boy can become ugly overnight if there is no kindness in his eyes.

"Mark my words, Sheindel," Tante would continue, "love is not a magic potion, and despite the fairy tales that people would have you believe, a frog cannot become a prince."

It is many years since Tante passed away, but experience has taught me that her theories were more often right than wrong. For better or worse, people are the products of their past, and despite the best of intentions, it is very difficult to unlearn patterns acquired in childhood. While it is possible to master a new subject, character changes are almost impossible to effectuate. I have seen individuals succeed in absorbing new ideas, and even in adopting new lifestyles, but I have seldom seen the transformation of a personality.

As difficult as it may be to accept the finality of this assertion, nevertheless it is best that we come to grips with it if we want to avoid pain in marriage. The very acts, the very expressions, that in our youth we found intolerable in our parents, become so deeply embedded in our psyches that despite ourselves, we tend to repeat them.

What emerges here is a sad, painful fact. Education cannot alter even one family problem. People who come from homes where dissension is the daily fare will not only perpetuate these conflicts, but unfortunately, will most likely transmit them to their progeny. Weaknesses as well as strengths are passed on from generation to generation. Moreover, family strife recognizes no social or cultural barriers. A doctor and a porter will experience the same ugly scenes in their homes if their backgrounds are conflict ridden. Lifestyles may change, but basic character traits remain immutable. Even in cases where it may appear that change has been effectuated, that after years of therapy a transformation has taken place, close scrutiny will reveal that these changes are purely cosmetic, and in moments of crisis, the old characteristics will quickly resurface. Admittedly, the idea that we are the products of our parents' neuroses is difficult to accept. If, however, we wish to avoid serious problems, it is best that we confront this reality. As Tante put it, to marry someone in the hope of changing him afterward is asking for trouble.

If Tante prized good character and a compassionate heart above all else, it is because she learned her lesson well from our father Abraham, who taught us that these were the essential ingredients for an enduring and stable family life. In seeking a wife for his son, the patriarch's primary concern was that the maiden come from a fine background, that she have been raised among people who were merciful and kindhearted, for he knew that if these traits were not acquired in early childhood, they could never be learned in later years. Philosophies, rituals, and ceremonies can all be studied, but a kind heart must be molded and shaped from infancy on. It was this awareness that prompted Abraham to subject his loyal servant Eliezer to a long and treacherous journey in order to find a wife for Isaac. In commissioning Eliezer to act as a *shadchan*, Abraham made him swear that he would never consider a Canaanite girl, for the spirit of Canaan was the spirit of Sodom and Gomorrah, where cruelty and viciousness were the daily fare. Abraham knew that a girl raised in such an atmosphere would have a heart of stone which even an Isaac would not be able to melt.

Eliezer, who was fully attuned to his master's thoughts, understood all this, and therefore made loving kindness the yardstick by which he would recognize the girl intended for the son of the patriarch.

"If I can find a girl," Eliezer prayed, "who will have the generosity of soul, not only to offer me, a stranger, some drink, but to water my camels as well, then I will know that I have found the girl who is worthy of Isaac."

It is important to bear in mind that in those days, drawing water from a well, especially for ten thirsty camels, was not quite the same as taking a bottle of pop from a refrigerator. It was not only arduous, back-breaking work, but expensive as well, for water was not free. Rebecca not only lived up to Eliezer's expectations, but she surpassed them, for in addition to offering Eliezer and his camels water, she also extended the hospitality of her home. When Eliezer saw this, he bowed his head in thanksgiving. He knew that he had found a maiden who would be a loving wife to Isaac, and more, would be worthy of becoming a mother in the tradition of Sarah, the first to lay the foundations of Jewish family life.

These eternal insights were transmitted to Sheindel by our family so that she might be able to build a home in the spirit of our ancestors.

It never occurred to me that there was anything extraordinary in the way in which Sheindel was prepared for marriage or in the manner in which she found her mate. Only years later did I realize that had Sheindel been Sue, born in

America and living alone in the big city, chances are that she would have spent her free hours scrambling for dates at singles' bars or similar places. If she had some relatives in the city, and if they were exceptionally nice, from time to time they might have spoken to her on the phone and invited her to dinner. But no one would have thought it proper to discuss her private life with her. Etiquette dictates that you mind your own business and not get involved in the personal affairs of others. This unwritten law is the gentleman's agreement which sets the tenor of American family life.

So, while Sue would have introduced her boyfriend to her family, they would most likely have refrained from making comments. This was strictly Sue's affair, and it was not for them to say whether they liked him or not.

There is an element of selfishness to this "live and let live" attitude. It is not always respect for the independence of others that prompts silence. Equally important is the fear of being involved, of being burdened by someone else's problems, of being blamed if things don't work out. And yet, that's the stuff that families are made of, helping, caring, and showing the way.

Sue's culture denied her such supportive guidance. Sheindel, on the other hand, never felt forsaken. Despite the fact that her family had perished in Auschwitz, she found a second home with us. Her problems became our problems, her happiness our joy. We made sure that she did not feel lonely or unwanted, and tried to spare her the humiliation of running to resorts and other such places, where she would be looked upon as so much merchandise, part of the sexual rat race.

Now perhaps you will protest that Sheindel was pressured into marriage. But that was not the case at all. While her upbringing conditioned her to regard the centrality of marriage as her ultimate goal in life, she was cautioned time and again not to settle for someone who was not of her choosing. Nor was this attitude peculiar to our family. All tradition-minded Jews raise their children by these very same dictates. And once again, the precedent was set by the Bible: Even as Rebecca had to consent to marry Isaac of her own free will, so our rabbis prescribed that all young people be given the same option and not be forced into marriage.

From the love story of Isaac and Rebecca, Sheindel learned to mistrust the overromanticized American way, and to recognize the pitfalls inherent in a union based on casual infatuation. Sheindel perceived that the "high" of love at first sight has no place to go but down. If everything is experienced prior to marriage (as it generally is nowadays), there is no room to develop and grow, there is nothing to build on, nothing to anticipate, nothing to sustain the relationship. She learned that love comes to its fullest realization after marriage, after two personalities are merged into one through *shared values and commitment.* It is written that only following marriage did Isaac's love for Rebecca truly blossom, for the more he shared with Rebecca, the closer he drew to her, the more he sacrificed for her, the more precious she became in his sight.

Sheindel perceived that if her marriage was to be marked by such dynamic love, she, too, would have to find someone with whom she could share common goals, someone who would understand that marriage meant not only a personal relationship, but a commitment through which the immortality of a nation could be guaranteed.

The architects of our people were not monarchs, politicians, or rabbis, but patriarchs and matriarchs, fathers and mothers. Our religion is a home- rather than a synagogue-centered faith. Our Seders, Sabbaths, rituals, and ceremonies are all observed within the confines of the family, and it is largely because of this that we have placed such strong emphasis on finding mates for our children who have the characteristics of compassion and goodness, for such traits are the prerequisites to creating stable homes where *shalom bayit*, peace and harmony, reign.

While peace and harmony is the literal translation of *shalom bayit*, the term has a far more profound implication. It connotes a love steeped in reverence, a genuine concern for one's mate, and a total commitment to one's children— values which are fundamental to the traditional Jewish home.

But if goodness and compassion are the foundation upon which a meaningful and lasting family life is built, and if such characteristics are hereditary, then what hope is there for those who come from troubled backgrounds? Are they bound to repeat the mistakes of their parents?

The answer is a resounding "NO!", for in the final analysis, every man can control his own destiny, and our Torah shows us the way. Our Biblical laws create the structure through which we can reshape our personalities and acquire new traits. To succeed, we must only temporarily suspend our feelings and allow the life-generating forces of the Commandments to take over and refine us.

Let us, for example, focus on a man whose selfishness inhibits him from being considerate of his family. He claims he would like to be generous, but he cannot, it's antithetic to his nature. Let such a man bend his will and follow the laws of the Torah which deal with family relationships. At first, each act of kindness will be painfully difficult. At times, he may even feel as though he were putting on an act. But eventually, that acting will become second nature and make him a better husband and father.

This holds true in every area. A man must only open himself to G-d's Commandments and he will discover that the transformation which had once seemed so unattainable can miraculously take place.

I have seldom seen this method fail. We need only the structure to make the change, and the Torah provides us with it. It regulates every moment of our day. There are 613 do's and don't's to remind us of our duty to our family, to our people, to our G-d. Already at the doorpost there is the emblem which marks the home. The *mezuzah*, which contains the immortal words "Hear O Israel, the L-rd our G-d, the L-rd is One," proclaims that this house is linked to an eternal heritage and G-d Himself is its Guardian. Here, time itself is elevated. Days are sanctified by holidays and Sabbaths, and every meal becomes a Divine service. Voices are not raised and curses are not heard, for a spirit of moral refinement prevails. Children are taught the art of hospitality, to consider the needs of others before their own, but perhaps most significant of all, the books of the Bible are not permitted to gather dust. They call out to the members of the family, "Study us and we shall show you the way."

And indeed, the Torah has shown us the way. It has rendered our homes impervious to the onslaughts of the outside world, protected our families from the corrosive pressures of society, and above all, enabled us to overcome our weaknesses so that we might bequeath to our children a heritage of honor, righteousness, and love. But where such guidance is missing, where homes are not insulated by Biblical values, insidious influences can attack like an army of termites and eat away at the very fabric of family life.

I had occasion to visit such a home. My host, a noted surgeon, who was also an art collector of sorts, gave me a tour of his house and proudly showed off his collection. When we reached the den I felt terribly uncomfortable, not only for myself, but also for his two little boys who were tagging along. One entire wall above the bar was paneled with a huge and explicit collage cut from *Playboy* centerfolds.

He must have sensed my embarrassment, because suddenly, he made an attempt to explain.

"Things are different today," he said. "I think we have a

much healthier attitude toward sex than our parents did. When I was a kid, I was always made to feel guilty. But take my boys, they're so used to seeing such pictures that it doesn't even bother them."

"You will forgive me," I said, trying hard not to be rude, "but I don't see anything healthy about children being used to pornography."

And with that, I went on to explain that the guilt to which he referred was, in essence, a blessing in disguise, which makes us blush in embarrassment and enables us to differentiate between right and wrong. But the moment we can no longer evoke such emotions, the moment we casually accept the degeneracy that surrounds us, that moment we also become a part of it.

Admittedly, a *Playboy* collage is not the typical decor of middle America, but *Playboy* magazines *are*, and in the final analysis, it makes little difference whether a picture hangs on a wall or lies on a magazine rack. The very fact that it is brought into the home conveys the parents' attitude to children.

You might, of course, argue that in our violent and sex-saturated society it is unrealistic to expect youngsters to remain untainted. But surprisingly, they can cope with the outside environment provided that their own homes remain inviolate, that they have fathers and mothers to whom they can relate with respect. As long as the mores of the street are not the mores of the home, children will be able to maintain a sense of balance. Even if they should drift, their guilt will leave them restless and prod them to return to those ideals which they had absorbed in their home environment.

Our tradition does not advocate the suppression or denial of sex. We do not subscribe to Victorian prudery, but if children are to be imbued with timeless values, parents will have to conduct themselves accordingly. It is important to remember that there is a great difference between love and sex, for while an expression of love between mother and father strengthens a child's sense of security, open manifestations of sex are demoralizing and corruptive.

When discussing this subject at one of my lectures, a lady in the audience objected. Although she agreed in principle, she considered my attitude unrealistic. She felt that in this day and age, there was no way to isolate children from pernicious influences. I agreed with her. There *is* no way. But that is precisely why parents have to become role models for their children to emulate.

Alas, corruption and immorality have been with us from time immemorial; over the years, only the names and places have changed. Already in Egypt, our ancestors had to grapple with decadence. The Bible teaches us that there were forty-nine levels of degeneracy there, the likes of which even Times Square has been unable to duplicate, yet it is written that Joseph never succumbed. Betrayed by his brethren, the only Jew in Egypt, Joseph had probably more to overcome than any young person today, and yet he withstood the enticements of his society because embedded in his soul was an image, the image of his father, whose life was a symbol of sanctity, reverence, and honor, and it was that image that enabled Joseph to prevail.

Whether we as parents have succeeded in imparting such an image to our own children can easily be determined. We must only ask ourselves what memories they will retain after we are gone. What image will they conjure up? How will they remember us?

No child can be fortified by memories of shopping trips, vacations, tennis, golf, or gourmet dinners. None of these experiences can communicate lasting ideals that ennoble or fortify. But that which is anchored to timeless values, that which comes from G-d transcends the generations and remains long after the parent is gone. How far-reaching such parental influence can be (even in the early years of life) was impressed upon me by a father who came to make Bar Mitzva arrangements for his son.

In conversation, he related that he had lost his own dad when he was only five years old. Although his mother had told him that his father had been a very devoted family man who spent a great deal of time playing with his children, regrettably he had no recollection of it.

But there was one thing he *did* remember. Every Friday night he would wait by the window for his father to come home from synagogue and say *kiddush*, a blessing over the wine.

The parties, the excursions, had all evaporated. Only the memory of his father's *kiddush* remained, and it was this memory that brought him to our door and inspired him to impart a legacy to his son as well.

Only such memories can sustain, only such memories can bring the Kevins back to their heritage.

> Except that the L-rd buildeth the house
> In vain do they that labor buildeth it.
>
> *Psalm 127*

A story is told of a renowned rabbi in Russia who was a quiet, humble, unassuming man. Many years passed before he and his wife were blessed with a family, but when his first son was born, his entire personality changed. No longer did he pronounce the blessings in a whisper. His voice resounded through the house as he proclaimed his prayers.

His wife was at a loss to understand this change. "Why," she asked him one day, "do you recite your prayers so loudly? What has happened to you since the baby was born?"

"Today, things are different," he explained. "Before I became a father, the blessings I pronounced were a matter between myself and G-d, but today, there are little eyes watching, little ears listening. *Today, I am transmitting something to the future.*"

That awareness is what parenting is all about. The true measure of a man is not determined by the manner in which he conducts his business, or by the way he communicates with his friends, but by the way he relates to his family, to his wife and children. Perhaps the most difficult task of a human being is to achieve success in this area. Nevertheless, we must attempt to rise to that challenge, for that's what life is all about. To be a father, to be a mother, to build a family.

🐛

five

FINDING HAPPINESS

NOWADAYS, IT IS THE rare parent who is willing to live with
the constant awareness that little eyes are watching and little
ears are listening. Today we are encouraged to think of ourselves first, and only then consider the needs of our children.

Perhaps the most classic example of this conflict between
family and self is the film *Kramer vs. Kramer.* In true contemporary style, Mrs. Kramer abandons her husband and
child to pursue her own self-interest, and in a pathetic letter
to her little boy writes, "Darling, I will always be your
mommy from long distance."

For the next two years, Mrs. Kramer devotes herself to
her much longed-for career, and although she is successful, it
does not bring her fulfillment. Broken and disillusioned, she
tries to recapture the joy she once had.

"Now I know what I want," she tells her husband.

"What?" he asks intently.

"I want to be a mother, I want my child," she pleads.

But alas, she makes this discovery too late.

Nor does Mr. Kramer fare much better. He, too, is convinced that personal achievement takes precedence over
family, only to find that he would gladly forgo his much cov-
eted promotion for the simple joy of being with his little boy.

But the damage has already been done, and the pain they each suffer can never be erased.

The tragedy of twentieth-century America: the breakdown of our families.

A distinguished member of the Sephardic Jewish community (whom I shall refer to as Jack) called me for an urgent consultation. In the course of my work, I had always enjoyed a warm relationship with members of this group and admired their loyalty to tradition. I tried to give Jack an immediate appointment, and since that evening I was scheduled to speak at a New York City college, I suggested he meet me there.

My lecture ran much longer than anticipated. The students kept raising all sorts of questions, and before I knew it, the caretaker came to shut the lights and tell us that he would have to close up. I felt awful. Jack had sat through the entire discussion with great patience, and here we were, being pushed out the door. I apologized, but he was most gracious. "It's more important for you to talk to young people. I can tell you my story as we walk. I just need a few minutes."

It was one of those bitter cold nights, when the wind blew mercilessly and tore right through your coat. But somehow, I managed to forget my freezing hands and feet and became fully engrossed in Jack's story.

"I just threw out my son," he announced. "I told him that I don't give a damn if he never comes home."

At this point, he paused, as if expecting me to protest.

"You think that a terrible thing for a father to do? Believe me, it hurts me much more than it will ever hurt him. But I had no choice. I am a father and I have my responsibilities."

Jack was a tall, imposing figure, with a shock of silver-gray hair and an authoritative bearing. And yet, there was a certain softness in his eyes which betrayed his sensitivity. He spoke with intensity and kept lighting one cigarette after another.

"I set him up in business," he went on, "and when he got married, I helped him buy a house. I'm not telling you this because I feel I deserve credit, any father would do the same, but I want you to understand the background," he said matter of factly.

"The girl he married was not Sephardic. To tell the truth, I would have preferred that he marry someone from our own community, but if he was happy, it was okay with me. It's ten years now, Rebbetzin. There are three beautiful children, and as far as I knew, everything was going well.

"Then, a few weeks ago, the trouble started. Bobby came into my office to make his big announcement. 'Dad,' he said, 'I'm getting a divorce.'

"His words hit me like a ton of bricks, but he just stood there telling me that he had to look out for his own happiness. I lost my temper. Here was a grown man, planning to abandon three little children, giving me all this crap about finding his own happiness.

"I tried to reason with him. 'Your wife is a good woman,' I said, 'you have three terrific kids. For G-d's sake, don't let anyone come between you.'

"But he refused to listen, and kept insisting that his break-up had nothing to do with another woman. And as far as the children were concerned, that to him was simple, they would just have to learn to manage. But I couldn't let go." Jack went on, "I had to get to the bottom of it and find out what had gotten into him."

Obviously agitated, Jack now stopped to light another cigarette. "Would you believe that the bum actually had the nerve to tell me that he was breaking up his marriage because his wife was cold!

" 'Cold,' " I said to him. 'Well, how the hell do you know that your mother wasn't cold? But damn you, did I leave her? Did I forsake you and your brothers?'

"I told my son that I'd had more chances to play around than he could ever have dreamt of, but I knew what it meant to be a father, and that to me always came first. I knew that if I brought children into the world, I had to give them a chance to be raised in a home with both parents. But my Bobby thinks he's hot stuff and not bound by any such responsibilities.

"So what could I do?" Jack now asked rhetorically. "I'm not a young man anymore, and here I have to become a father again. After all, I can't abandon those kids. You're my last hope, Rebbetzin. Would you call my son and remind him that three little children are waiting for their daddy to come home?"

While we were talking, it had started to snow, but I hardly noticed it. I was totally taken by this man, who in his own way captured the essence of the greatest of human challenges: to be a father, to nurture children.

But why didn't his son understand? Why didn't he follow in his father's footsteps? To put it down to assimilation would, of course, be the easy way out. But it was not quite as simple as that. Bobby was a product of the Sephardic Jewish community, in which tradition is paramount, especially as regards family life. So what went wrong? Why did Bobby rebel? Why did he turn his back on his wife and children?

The problem was especially irksome since I have maintained throughout that children are a reflection of their homes and will emulate the example set by their parents. If Bobby saw his father sacrifice, why didn't he do the same? What prompted him to depart from his family's way?

The spoiling of Bobby and his generation has deep roots in our American culture and can be traced all the way back to the founding fathers, who declared the pursuit of happiness an *inalienable right*. Obviously, their proclamation was motivated by the best of intentions, but that in no way prevented future generations from perverting it. To be sure, when they authored their declaration, they would never have imagined that one day fathers like Bobby would abandon their families and try to justify their lack of responsibility by referring to that "inalienable right," or that they would make the pursuit of happiness their national pastime.

From early childhood, American youth are trained to regard this inalienable right as their prerogative. The very quality of their education is influenced by it. It is not conduct or morals that are salient to the parents. More significant is their child's emotional adjustment. "I want my son to be happy in school," or "I want him to enjoy his classes" have become their popular catch phrases. Children have only to complain about a teacher not relating or about a subject not being sufficiently stimulating to have their parents rally to their side. And the formula is equally effective when applied in reverse, when children complain that it is *their parents* who are neglecting them. Whichever way it goes, the youngsters quickly discover that it is possible to shirk all responsibility by pitting parents against teachers and vice versa.

I have tried to imagine what my own mother's reaction would have been if, as a child, I had complained in a similar vein. "Why should you enjoy your classes?" she probably would have said. "You're not going to school for fun, but to learn. There are a lot of things in life you won't enjoy, but you have to do them regardless. There is such a thing as responsibility."

But my mother's attitude is the exception, not the norm, for our society. We have been led to believe that self-gratification takes precedence over duty, that the end goal of all our endeavors must be happiness, and everything in our culture, from the media, to business, to education, reinforces this idea.

The seduction starts at an early age, when a bewitching voice promises little tots that they need only get mommy to buy them a certain toy to be the happiest of children. The toy is bought, but the promised transformation never takes place. The voice, however, remains relentless.

With the passage of time, the toy is exchanged for a stereo, a sports car, a house in the suburbs, or a vacation in an exotic spot. There is always something new being promised, but after the product has been acquired, a let-down always sets in, for no matter how much we have, there is always something more we need. We are like children, who in our innocence think that if we could only get up in a plane, we would be able to touch the sky. But once we get up there, the sky remains as distant as ever.

"When will you have enough? When will you be satisfied?" I once asked an acquaintance who was always on the run.

"You make me sound greedy," he said resentfully, "and that's not the case at all. I just want to be happy."

I proceeded to tell him about the time I broke my finger. We couldn't get hold of a doctor, so my husband rushed me to the emergency room of a nearby hospital. A terrible scene greeted us there. People suffering from lacerations, burns, gunshot wounds, and every other imaginable ailment. While I waited my turn, a young woman with a baby in her arms ran in. Her child had fallen down a flight of stairs and blood was gushing from his head.

The woman took a seat next to me, her tears mingling with those of her baby. I tried to reassure her, but she mumbled something incoherent, and pointed to a sign above the receptionist's window. "Happiness," the sign read, "is like a butterfly that lights on your shoulder. No sooner do you realize that it's there than it flies away."

"I guess my butterfly just flew away," the woman whispered.

"Did it ever occur to you," I now said to my friend, "that at this very moment there might be a butterfly resting on your shoulder, but at the rate you're going, by the time you become aware of it, it will have flown away?"

Neither my friend nor Bobby recognized the moment when the butterfly was theirs. It was only in reminiscing about the past that they came to value the joy they once had.

Time and again, in unguarded moments, divorced men and women have confided to me that if they had it to do over again, they would probably have stayed married to their original mates. Marriage is at best difficult, and those who wish to succeed at it must be prepared to work hard. But no one ever bothered to impress this upon Bobby, no one bothered to explain to him that while marriage would bring him satisfaction, it would also present him with a new set of challenges which at times would be so overwhelming that they would make him want to run.

Nor did anyone bother to point out that the perfect sexual relationships that he read about were not based on reality, but were the fantasies of writers who exploit people's needs. Bobby never realized that romance and marriage were incompatible, that one thrived on mystery, while the other was rooted in the stark reality of everyday living. Bobby truly believed that he had only to fall in love in order to live happily ever after, and this belief was fed by his culture.

The advertisements depicting young marrieds somehow always seemed to focus on the romantic. No matter what they were doing, they always had that "certain look" which told the world that to be married is to be divinely happy.

Bobby would vehemently deny that he had been duped by this romantic nonsense. But despite his protestations, the insidious influences were there.

Reality hit him hard, and he was not prepared to cope with it. He felt choked by the grinding monotony of family life. He was not prepared for kids who whine, whose noses always seem to be running, whose diapers need constant changing, and who deprive him of his freedom. His wife, too, was dissatisfied, and felt that she got the raw end of the deal, and they drew further and further apart, until he became convinced that she was cold.

Bobby is unhappy. He sees his life slipping away, and becomes a prime candidate for another woman or some other form of escape. Fortified by the latest best sellers which exhort him to look out for number one, Bobby is ready to run. The words keep echoing in his mind: "These are your best years. You're only young once. Don't let anyone deprive you of your inalienable rights."

Bobby is a product of his society, and there is no way to warn him that the happiness he seeks does not exist, that more important than finding the right partner is *being* the right partner. There is no one to tell him that he will have to pay a terrible price for his freedom, that instead of resolving his difficulties, divorce might just open a Pandora's box and turn out to be no different than exchanging measles for chicken pox.

Nor is it possible to appeal to Bobby's conscience. In a society in which happiness is regarded as the ultimate goal, morality and absolutes become blurred. Bobby remembers his school lessons well. It is not his conduct that is salient, but his emotional adjustment.

Bobby cannot anticipate the abject loneliness that awaits him in his new bachelor pad, the monotony of eating in public places, or the sexual rat-race of the singles world. Bobby cannot allow himself to get embroiled in the feelings of his children, who will now see him and his ex-wife scrambling for dates, running off with girlfriends and boyfriends. He is assured that given time, they will learn to adjust, and he must now consider his own welfare.

I would have liked to tell Bobby the story of a divorced man who came to my office and told me about the trouble he was having with his children. The youngsters (who were in his ex-wife's custody) didn't like his new girlfriend, and there was constant bickering.

"I'm sure that my ex is the one who's riling them up against her, but I'm not going to let them get away with it," he announced. "I can't let them run my life."

And then he went on to tell me about what had happened that past Sunday evening.

"Well, it was my turn to take the kids, so I arranged for all of us to go out to dinner. But would you believe it, they had a conspiracy going to give my girl a hard time. So I said to them, 'Okay, kids, if that's the way it's going to be, we're going right home.'

"I called over the maître d', tipped him, and told him that we'd be leaving without dinner. The kids were furious, but I couldn't care less. I wasn't going to stand for any of it. They threatened to tell the story to our therapist, so I said, 'Go right ahead.'

"But guess what?" the man said triumphantly. "The therapist sided with me! He told the kids in plain English that they'd better toe the mark, or else they might just wind up losing a father."

I didn't know whether to laugh or cry. Where do you start explaining? How do you make a man see the absurdity of his situation? A father vying with his children for approval from the shrink!

"Did you ever stop to consider," I asked, "how your children read this whole scene? Did it ever occur to you that what you and your therapist are communicating to your kids is that this girl is more important to you than they could ever hope to be?"

"I'm sorry," he protested, missing my point entirely, "the kids behaved rudely, and had to be taught proper manners."

"I would fully agree with you," I said, "if you had taught them just that. But you didn't teach them manners. You didn't teach them consideration for others. The only lesson that you conveyed was selfishness: 'My girl and I come first, and if you kids interfere with our happiness, you'll just have to get out.'

"Your divorce itself was a bitter pill for your children to swallow. Why exacerbate their pain by flaunting the woman who has taken their mother's place? Don't you understand?" I went on. "Precisely because you are divorced, your children need assurance that your love shall remain steadfast and no one will ever come between you."

But apart from the harm rendered to his children, the man himself incurred the greatest punishment, for while he may have found a new wife, his son and daughter were lost in the process.

A man's emotional well-being is very much like his physical health. Just as he cannot amputate a portion of his body without feeling pain, so he cannot cut himself off from his loved ones without suffering. Personal happiness cannot be realized if it does not take into consideration these needs.

It is for this reason that in Jewish life, when extending greetings for the coming year, we use the term, *Shana Tova*, meaning, "Have a good year," rather than "Have a happy New Year," for we understand that the happiness we hope for can only be realized through goodness, through the fulfillment of our responsibilities, through the kindness that we extend to those who are near and dear to us.

Had Bobby and his generation been trained to value goodness above happiness, self-renunciation above self-indulgence, they would have discovered the simple joys of life which render dividends in contentment and blessing. But they were never taught to sacrifice or to place another's needs above their own. All their emotional resources were invested in themselves, they always had to be "number one."

It is this obsession with self which was at the root of Bobby's neuroses. He couldn't afford to admit to failure and had a need to blame others for his deficiencies. It's not *he* who failed, it was his wife who was cold. It's not *he* who fell short, but his family who didn't understand. His self-infatuation became crippling, rendering him incapable of making the lasting commitments required in marriage, for no matter how much Bobby had, he was consumed by a nagging suspicion that he was missing something, that he was no longer "number one."

There is no one to tell him that "number one" is reserved for the Only One, the Almighty G-d Himself, that if a man is to find happiness, he must lost himself in the needs of others, for the more he concentrates on his own desires, the greater his despondency will become.

Not being able to reach beyond himself, Bobby had no peace. He confused happiness with fun, and pursued it with a vengeance. It was not only distraction that he sought, but escape. Saturday night on the town became his religious rite. Even if he had no place to go, he had to get into the car just to take a ride, to get away. But should you have caught him in a quiet moment, as I did, you would have discovered that his raucous laughter and glued-on smile masked a frightened and lonely heart.

Bobby walked out on his family, but his dreams of happiness continued to elude him, and after a while the realization hit him that there was no place left to run, that if he couldn't find happiness within himself, he probably would never find it anywhere. Fortunately for him, his family's patience and perseverance enabled him to return to his wife and children before it was too late. But alas, not everyone is so favored.

For most, the realization that they have been touched by a butterfly comes too late, when that butterfly has already flown away.

"What is happiness?" I once asked my father, and immediately he answered by quoting from the Bible, "Happy is the man whose children sit around his table like magnificent olive plants" (*Psalm 128:3*).

The way my mother and father looked at us, the way they pronounced our names, told us that, indeed, we were their "magnificent olive plants," the sum total of their joy. This knowledge was dynamic, for it not only gave my parents happiness, but it infused us with happiness as well. We had few material possessions, but somehow we children never felt deprived. Even when we first came to this country and lived in a dilapidated, cramped basement apartment, it never occurred to us that we were poor, although all the other children on our block lived in comparatively spacious homes.

For years, I wore hand-me-downs. We simply could not afford anything new. But I never thought that my friends were better off than I was. As a matter of fact, there were times when I was convinced that in many ways I was the richest kid on the block, the only one who never had any problems at home, and the only one who did not have to ask permission to go to the corner candy store for a comic book or a piece of gum. We never received an allowance. Whatever money we needed, we were free to take from the dresser drawer in which my parents kept whatever cash there was in the house. My brothers and I never abused this privilege, but were eager to add our own meager earnings (from babysitting or other chores) to that little box in the drawer.

Nowadays, children are denied such joyous experience. Parental concern that children not be taken advantage of, that they be self-assertive, renders them selfish and ungenerous.

"Don't be a fool. Don't do anything unless you get paid for it," is our advice to our enterprising youngsters, and when they take that lesson a step further and demand payment for helping around the house, we take pride in their cleverness.

The moment, however, that a child is paid for washing daddy's car or for babysitting for a younger sibling, his relationship to his family becomes calculating. He is denied the happiness which comes with the giving of self, and the knowledge that through his efforts, a loved one has been helped. Cold cash can never equal the reward of a mother's smile or a father's approving nod, which assure the child that he is appreciated.

This inability to give without expecting something in return mars all our relationships, leaves us suspicious, fearful that we are being had, and prevents us from reaching out beyond ourselves, which is the pre-condition to finding happiness.

Happiness can never be a pursuit or an end in itself. Rather, it must be the by-product of a certain way of life that is based upon kindness and consideration, giving and sharing.

Even as the founders of our republic legislated happiness as an inalienable right, so the fathers of our Jewish people considered happiness the cultivation of a particular attitude:

"Who can be termed a happy man?" they asked.

"He who is content with his lot" (*Ethics of the Fathers*, Chapter 4:1).

Our fathers understood the complex nature of man who always yearns to possess more, who believes that the grass is greener on the other side, and who, despite his attainments, remains dissatisfied. This discontent is his undoing, and precludes him from taking pleasure in the simple blessings of life. In vain do we legislate happiness for him. It is not rights that he lacks, but the ability to enjoy them. It is not possessing more, but *being* more that is his problem, and it is not quantity, but rather the quality of life that must become his quest.

It is told that an unhappy man once consulted his rabbi. "How can I overcome my feelings?" he asked. "No matter what I do, there is always something bothering me. I always feel dissatisfied."

The rabbi pondered the problem for a while. "I cannot help you," he said, "but there is a wise old sage who lives in a nearby town. He will be able to guide you."

And so, the man set out to find the sage. But when he arrived at the town in which the holy man was supposed to live, he could not locate him, no one had ever even heard of him. Finally, someone suggested that he try a broken-down house at the outskirts of the village.

The man couldn't understand it. How could someone who lived in an old, broken-down shanty give him advice on happiness? But since those were the specific instructions of his rabbi, he felt he had to see it through.

When he arrived at the house, he was more than ever convinced that the whole thing was a horrible mistake. The house was completely barren. Poverty hung so heavily in the air that you could almost touch it. The sage whom he had been told to seek out was sitting on a broken chair, studying ancient books. The man felt ridiculous asking his question. It would be insulting to remind this man of his abject misery. But since he had come this far, he would follow his rabbi's counsel.

"I was sent to you," he began feebly, "by my rabbi, who told me that you would be able to advise me how to overcome my feelings of unhappiness."

The sage looked up from his books with a quizzical expression. He shook his head in wonderment. "I don't understand why your rabbi thought I could help you. I really wouldn't know how to deal with such feelings, *Baruch Hashem,* blessed be G-d, I cannot recall ever experiencing unhappiness."

It took a few moments for the man to digest fully the import of the sage's words, and then he recalled the timeless teachings of his faith:

Who is a happy man?
He who is content with his lot.

This pronouncement of *Baruch Hashem,* blessed be G-d, was more than a mere formality, for it enabled our people to develop that all-important attitude of contentment which our sages teach is the basis of happiness. It reminded us that G-d was always there, that He was guiding our destiny and knew what was best for our welfare. Even when at times we did not understand, that realization gave us confidence and strength.

It's not that we viewed life through rose-colored glasses. We anticipated problems, and when trouble came our way, we hurt as much as the next person. Nevertheless, the knowledge that there was a greater power above us who authored, directed, and orchestrated our lives, enabled us to accept our fate without resentment. The simple pronouncement of *Baruch Hashem,* blessed be G-d, enabled us to maintain a positive attitude, free of bitterness.

One of our organization's more active members approached me about a growing schism between herself and her sister. When I met the sister weeks later, I understood the source of the problem. Whereas my friend was attractive and vivacious, the sister was homely and cynical. There was no talking to her, she was full of hatred. First, she hated G-d, who had favored her sister over her. Then she hated her parents, whom she blamed for her shortcomings, and then she hated her sister for being so popular and successful. Her hatred was so all-consuming that it poisoned her entire personality.

There was no denying that she had cause for resentment. Why had her sister been so blessed and she so deprived?

But had she understood the meaning of *Baruch Hashem*, blessed be G-d for what I have, she would have drawn solace from the knowledge that her features were the creation of the Almighty, who in His infinite wisdom always has a reason for doing what He does. True, that awareness would not have changed her features, but it certainly would have altered her appearance and removed the cold hostility from her eyes and the tight bitterness from around her mouth. Instead of wallowing in self-pity, she could have made the most of what she *did* have.

Now, this in no way implies that we should passively resign ourselves to our fate. As youngsters, we were taught never to be complacent, never to rely on miracles. We had to do our part, and if despite all our efforts, we failed, then and only then could we be content that we had exhausted all the means available to us, and things were not *bashert*, meant to be.

Bashert is a new concept which I have not yet introduced. It is a Yiddish word which is almost impossible to translate. It implies a faith that there is a Divine investment in our lives, that despite insurmountable obstacles, everything will somehow turn out right. *Bashert* prevented us from agonizing if things did not happen as anticipated. We knew that there was a reason for it. It was *bashert*. Even our prayers were affected by it. We were taught never to ask G-d for any specific thing, but rather, to beseech Him to guide us along the right path, for only He knew what was *bashert*, meant to be for us.

And so, when it came to major decisions in our lives, we always relied on Him, for how could we know with certitude what was to our benefit or what might spell our downfall?

One moment we would be positive that if we could only attain a certain goal our happiness would be complete, only to discover that what we wished for was our undoing.

Whenever I would think of the implications of *bashert*, I would think of Rabbi Akiva and feel fortified.

Rabbi Akiva took upon himself Jewish commitment very late in life. He was a poor, illiterate shepherd who, at the age of forty, began to learn the Hebrew alphabet. In his desire to study at the great Torah Academies, he undertook a long and treacherous journey. He traveled by donkey, and took all his possessions with him: his books, a candle by which he would study, and a rooster to awaken him in the early hours of the morning. As night fell, he became tired and hungry and decided to seek lodging in a small town. He knocked on the door of a little house, hoping to be allowed to stay the night. A woman opened the door, but just as quickly slammed it in his face. "Strangers are not welcome here," she exclaimed.

Taken aback by this lack of hospitality, Akiva became somewhat despondent, but he consoled himself with the thought that there must be some reason that this was happening. It must be *bashert* that he not spend the night in a warm house. So, wearily, he mounted his donkey and made for the forest where he spread a mat on the ground, lit a candle, opened one of his books, and began to study. Suddenly, he heard his donkey bray. There was a great uproar. Akiva ran toward his beast, but he was too late. A lion had come and devoured it. His luck seemed to be running out. Things were going from bad to worse. Now he would have to travel on foot, and who knows how long it would take him to get to the Academy?

But Akiva murmured to himself, *"Baruch Hashem,* blessed be G-d. Whatever He does is for the best. This too must be *bashert."*

He was about to return to his studies, when there was yet another disturbance. This time it was the cock who fell dead.

Was this the reward of a man who undertakes an arduous journey and sacrifices everything in order to become a Torah scholar?

Akiva could surely have become cynical and renounced his faith, but instead, he kindled his candle and continued on. But the wind blew so fiercely that it was impossible to keep the candle lit, and so, in sheer exhaustion, he fell asleep.

The following morning, he resumed his journey, stopping at the village where he had been refused lodging the night before. A horrible sight greeted him. Robbers had come during the night and plundered and destroyed everything in sight. With a heavy heart, Akiva whispered to himself, "G-d's guiding hand is always there. It was *bashert* that I was not extended hospitality in this house; it was *bashert* that I lost my donkey and rooster, and it was even *bashert* that the wind blew out my candle, for had the robbers found me, I would not be here now."

Akiva continued his journey, and as he walked he uttered a silent prayer, *"Baruch Hashem,* blessed be G-d, all that He does is for the best."

At one time or another, in our own way, we all experience the trials of Rabbi Akiva, when everything seems to be going against us and we feel we can no longer go on. At such times, we can resign ourselves to cynicism or find a measure of equanimity in the knowledge that G-d is there and somehow He will set it all to rights. It is this basic difference in attitude which enables one man to find happiness and proclaim *Baruch Hashem,* blessed be G-d, and another to remain a prisoner of his own bitterness.

To be able to accept our fate with dignity, to confront life in all its reality, and to know that even when we do not perceive Him, He is nevertheless there. If we can retain such faith, we will not be consumed by the constant gnawing worries that erode the mind, or by the greed that keeps inciting us to believe that we do not have enough. Instead of trying to escape reality, we will be able to confront life head on and echo the words of Akiva, *"Baruch Hashem,* blessed be G-d. He is my partner, and whatever He does must be for the best."

"Who is a happy man?" our fathers asked.

"He who is content with his lot."

six

LONELINESS

OUR UNREALISTIC EXPECTATIONS of happiness make us resentful of any misfortune that may come our way. Since we have been conditioned to believe that happiness is our inalienable right, we have difficulty coping when calamity strikes. We indulge in self-pity, and are convinced that we alone have been singled out for unfair treatment while others were allowed to get away. Feelings of isolation overwhelm us, and our loneliness is intensified because we have precious little to fall back on.

Our ancestors were better off. Whenever they felt troubled they looked to their past and found reassurance:

> Look unto the rock from whence you were hewn . . .
> Look unto your father Abraham and your mother Sarah who bore you . . .
>
> (*Isaiah* 51:1–2)

These immortal words of the prophet called out to them and lifted them up. They never felt quite alone or abandoned, because their past had become a source of strength from which they were able to draw. Equally sustaining was their perception of the future, their awareness that they had a responsibility to those who would yet come. Thus sandwiched between history and destiny, they were imbued with a sense of purpose and protected from the pain of loneliness.

But how can we protect ourselves today? How are we to overcome this malaise of our time?

Once again, the answer is family.

Members of a family are very much like passengers on a ship. None can act independently lest he endanger the lives of others, for were just one passenger to bore a hole under his seat, it is not only his life, but the lives of all those on board with him that would be jeopardized.

This awareness that one cannot act independently, that one's deeds and thoughts can actually affect others, is the best antidote to loneliness.

There are those, however, who will be unimpressed by such an analogy. They will shrug their shoulders and say, "No thanks. If that's how it's gotta be, I'd rather set sail alone and take my chances. I have enough trouble dealing with my own problems without having to be saddled with those of others."

Such an attitude is typical of our culture. It reflects an aversion to all entanglements and responsibilities. By setting sail alone, modern man not only invites loneliness, but he also jeopardizes his well-being, for the sea of life has turbulent waters, and even with the best laid plans, the going is bound to get rough. If, at such difficult moments, a man can no longer feel attached to someone, then he has no reason to go on. It becomes much simpler to let go and give up the fight.

It is only the awareness that there are others in his boat who count on him, who depend on him, that will enable him to summon the iron will to continue.

Delores and Walter are two people whose lives testify that in the last ditch it is only family that can pick you up.

Their story first came to my attention when, one morning, I opened the papers and there, staring right back at me, was a picture of Walter, who lived in the New Jersey community in which my husband had his first pulpit. A sordid tale unfolded. It appeared that Walter had been involved in a stock fraud. Not only was he accused of embezzling hundreds of thousands of dollars, investigation also revealed that he had been leading a double life. Unknown to his wife and four children, Walter had a second family living somewhere in New York City. Overnight, Delores discovered that for the past sixteen years she had been deceived by a horrible lie. On the day when Walter was taken to prison, Delores was left with exactly sixty-five dollars in her purse. The creditors took everything else. Lifelong friends on whom she felt she could depend turned against her. One of them even laid claim to her house. It was a horrible nightmare from which there was no awakening. Delores was all alone. Her world had caved in and she had only one wish left—to die, to just disappear.

She went into hiding. She could not bring herself to face people. It came to the point where she could not even bear to do her grocery shopping. Her four children stopped going to school. Everywhere they went, people were whispering behind their backs.

My own association with Delores had always been somewhat distant. She had not joined our congregation, so I never got to know her well. Still and all, I would have called her, but I was afraid that she might misinterpret my interest as idle curiosity, food for gossip.

I have always tried to follow the teaching of our sages, who advised us never to intrude on anyone in their hour of disgrace. Only very close friends should call at such times, and anyone outside of that intimate circle should have the good sense to keep away. Nevertheless, having heard that Delores had been left abandoned, I decided to give her a ring and tell her that I was there should she need me. But as I had anticipated, she was uncommunicative and rather cold.

I was therefore taken completely off guard when, a few

days later, I found Delores standing at my front door. I hardly recognized her. She had always been such an attractive woman, and suddenly, she had become haggard and old.

"Is it all right to come in? Maybe I don't have the right to walk into a rabbi's home," she stammered, choking on her words.

I ran down the steps and embraced her. For a long time, we just stood there, I rocking her trembling body, and she weeping hysterically.

"Rebbetzin," she sobbed, "my life is over. There is nothing, absolutely nothing to live for. I wish I could die, but damn it, I can't afford even that. It's strange, isn't it," she cried, "the grave is the only place where I could find some peace, but I have kids and somebody has to take care of them."

For a long time, I remained silent, waiting for her to get it all out. Then, slowly, I tried to calm her and give her some hope.

"Delores," I said, still holding her in my arms. "I know that it may be difficult for you to accept what I have to say, but please, dear, at least try. Do not think that I take your tragedy lightly, but despite everything, I tell you that all is not lost. I know that this may sound crazy, but you have two great gifts going for you, *children* and *time*. Right now, you may think that your children are only an added burden, but I'm telling you that they are your blessings who force you to keep your sanity until the second gift, time, takes over."

Delores looked at me uncomprehendingly.

"Be patient," I went on, "and you will discover that time is a wonderful healer. Nothing is forever, not even suffering. This may sound somewhat trite, but night is always followed by day, and eventually the sun does shine. You will see, Delores, that the sun will yet shine for you. Even though it's hard to believe it now, with every passing day, some of the sharpness of your pain will be dulled, until one day you will wake up and discover that you have started a new life."

But Delores just kept shaking her head in disbelief. My words seemed to make no impression at all.

"Look," I said finally, taking a strong hold of her shoulders, "you yourself admit that it was only your children who prevented you from ending it all. If not for your kids, you would probably never have made it to my door. That's the gift I'm talking about. Now just hang in there, and allow the second gift, time, to do its healing work."

Delores could not be consoled. "Rebbetzin," she protested, "you don't understand. That's not the answer. I don't want to live through my children. I don't want to be dependent on them. I want to live my own life, but now it's over. I have nothing, absolutely nothing."

"I do understand," I reassured her. "You want to have your own independent life. But is there any human being who is truly independent? If not for your children, for whom or what would you live? A job? A lover? Or even a husband? Would they lend greater meaning to your life than your own children?"

Delores stared at me in silence, but her eyes told me that I was finally getting through. We talked for a long time and as we spoke, she gained courage.

Slowly and painfully, Delores began to rebuild. She found a job, made new friends, and started the beginnings of a normal life again. There were some days that were more difficult than others, but then she would think of her children and they gave her the strength to go on.

While Delores was able to muster a semblance of hope from her children, Walter had absolutely nothing to latch onto. Shunned by his family and society, he was totally alone. The only thing separating him from death were the prison guards who kept him under constant surveillance after he was found trying to hang himself. Despite the fact that I had never really gotten to know Walter, in my mind's eye I kept seeing him locked behind bars, suffocating in his cell. After all, his face was not an anonymous blob, a mere picture in a newspaper; he was someone real whom I had seen in the neighborhood, walking his dog, mowing his lawn, and I felt that, if nothing else, I should at least make an attempt to communicate with him.

But when it came down to it, I felt idiotic. What could I possibly say that would make sense and not come off sounding patronizing? Besides, I rationalized, Walter was guilty and had to pay for his crime, so why should I get involved? Yet I knew that that was not the answer. Did not our Torah teach us that it was not the punishment of a man that G-d desires, but that he mend his ways, cleanse his heart, and start a new life? But in a prison cell, who would show Walter the way? Who would prevent him from becoming even more brutalized?

My husband and I agreed that we should at least try to write to him. But what to say remained a problem, especially since we knew that there was no family to keep his hopes up.

"Why don't you relate the experiences you had when you spoke at that prison in Israel?" my husband suggested. "That might just do the trick."

There is only one correctional facility for women in Israel, and fortunately, there are very few inmates there. But in a country as small as Israel, where citizens are regarded as family members, a great deal of effort is expended on rehabilitating them. And so it was that on one of my speaking tours, I was invited to address these women of Ramle Prison.

Now, if I had qualms about writing to Walter, you can well imagine how uneasy I felt about actually speaking in a prison. Yet I felt that I must try. As a lecturer, I hardly ever find myself at a loss for words, but here I was somewhat stymied. There was so much that I wanted to say, and yet I was also aware that one wrong word could easily demolish hearts that were already wounded. What could I possibly say that would not sound self-righteous or condescending?

We arrived at Ramle in the heat of a scorching summer day, accompanied by one of the directors of Israel's Radio News Service. We rang the bell over the great iron gates, and as they slowly opened, Barbara, who is normally very agile and quick on her feet, tripped and fell flat on her face.

Even as Barbara was cleansing her scrapes, it occurred to me that I had my speech. I proceeded to introduce her to the inmates and explained that in all the years that we had worked together, I had never seen her take a flop like that. Perhaps, I said, this happened here so that all of us might learn a lesson.

"Every man can fall, but the idea is to get up. We came here today so that, together, we might find the best way to do just that—to stand up and start all over again."

Of all my programs, perhaps that little speech in the dust of Ramle was my most moving experience. We stayed the entire afternoon. The women had myriad questions. They wanted to study, start classes, and find their way back to their heritage.

We were about to leave, when one of the girls approached me and pressed a piece of paper into my hand.

"Would you take it to Jerusalem," she asked, her eyes full of tears, "and place it in a crevice in the Western Wall?"

On the note were written the four most beautiful words that a human being can articulate. "Almighty G-d, forgive me," it read.

Four words that enable a man to look within his soul and start all over again.

Obviously, there was a great difference between those misguided girls at Ramle, who were driven by poverty and family problems into the streets, and Walter. Nevertheless, I took a gamble, and hoped that he would derive some inspiration from my story. As long as he had life, I wrote, even if it was in a dingy cell, he could learn to stand up and redress the wrong.

The path back, I conceded, would not be easy, for even should he be willing to make a fresh start, society would not be forgiving. His prison record would follow him like a sinister shadow for the rest of his life. No matter what he might do, there would always be a number attached to his name. But in the Heavenly Courts, such matters are judged differently. There, if a man truly repents, his forgiveness is complete. G-d actually erases a man's past and gives him a new lease on life.

I underlined two passages from the Bible for Walter to meditate on. The first was from *Isaiah* 1, and it testified that if a man wished, he could start all over again:

> Come now, let us reason together, sayeth the L-rd.
> Though your sins be red as scarlet,
> they can be made white as snow . . .
>
> *(Isaiah 1:18)*

The second passage was from *Psalm 27*, confirming that even if a man be abandoned by his earthly family, G-d never casts him off:

> Even if my father and mother shall forsake me,
> G-d shall gather me to Him.
> Hope in the L-rd, place your trust in Him
> and your heart shall be strengthened and given courage.
>
> *(Psalm 27:10)*

You need only seek out our Heavenly Father, keep His Commandments, and study the Bible, and He will show you the way.

> For the L-rd does not desire the death of the sinner,
> but that he depart from his ways.
>
> *(Ezekiel 33:11)*

Walter appeared very much touched by my concern, but he found the road to religion fraught with hardship. "I wish I could have faith," he wrote, "but it would be hypocritical for me to pretend that I believe in G-d when I don't."

I had always thought that in the foxhole there were no atheists, but Walter seemed to be the exception to the rule. Then, one day, we received a letter which indicated that something was finally happening.

"I'm praying and reading the Bible," he wrote. "I'm starting to stand up."

Well, I said to myself, it seems that the old adage is true after all. Ultimately, there comes a point when a man has no choice but to turn to G-d. Still, Walter took an inordinately long time to come around, perhaps even longer than someone who may have had a similar experience living in another culture.

The story of Walter and Delores could have happened in any generation and in any society. Greed and corruption are as old as time itself, yet there was something typically contemporary in the events that unfolded here. When Delores protested that she must live her own life, independent of her children, and when Walter declared himself incapable of turning to G-d, they were expressing distinctively American ideals of independence which are very much at the root of the loneliness afflicting our generation.

Even as the founding fathers of our republic declared the pursuit of happiness to be an inalienable right, so they designated independence a life goal to strive for. Philosophers and writers such as Jefferson, Emerson, Thoreau, Twain, and Hemingway all contributed to the formulation of this value system which exhalts the independence of the individual. Perhaps it was Emerson who had the greatest impact in shaping this ideology. He advised us to trust no one but ourselves and to make our own needs our priority. "Do your own thing," "Be your own man," "Assert yourself," is the stuff of which American dreams were made. The lone cowboy roaming the prairie, Horatio Alger, who was a self-made success, and John Henry, who was already self-sufficient at birth, are only a few examples of this American quest.

But Horatio Alger and John Henry are only legend, and to confuse them with reality is to encourage discontent. Just as the pursuit of happiness indulged Bobby's self-centeredness and ultimately contributed to his undoing, so the cult of independence rendered Delores lonely and frightened and Walter callous and corrupt. To them, independence implied that they stood alone, and they were certain and no one would ever want to sacrifice for them. To be sure, Delores and Walter were at opposite ends of the pole, but they were linked by a common value system which focused on the self. Delores actually believed that if she were to dedicate herself to her children, she would compromise her individuality, while Walter was convinced that no one gave a damn, and therefore, he could do as he pleased.

It was to eradicate this self-centeredness that G-d made man a dependent being who could find fulfillment only through dedication to others.

To embed this yearning in his heart, G-d originally created Man as one entity. Only later, when Man realized his own loneliness, did G-d divide him into two creatures, Adam and Eve.

Man, G-d teaches, can never be complete unless he is united with his partner. Therefore, family life is not an option, but a command which was called into being on the Sixth Day of Creation.

"It is not good for man to be alone . . . Therefore shall a man leave his mother and father and cleave unto his wife . . . Be fruitful and multiply and replenish the earth . . ." (*Genesis* 2:18, 24; 1:28).

G-d warned us that we cannot live in solitude, that we

must establish homes, give life to children, and yes, build families.

Despite the impressive theories advanced by our philosophers and educators, despite our American credo of independence, there is just no way we can defy this Divine law and proclaim ourselves self-sufficient. Family life is rooted in interdependence, in the awareness that we are all the components of a larger unit, that indeed, we are all passengers on a ship, and if we are to survive, we must accept responsibility for those who are on board with us.

Perhaps you will now understand why Delores's situation was so desperately hopeless. In other societies, a woman might have found solace and strength through her children, but Delores could take no comfort from them. Her culture demanded that she rely on no one but herself. To have admitted her need would have been to concede her weakness, and that she could not bear. It was only after I challenged her directly and stripped away all the sophisticated, meaningless verbiage surrounding independence that she realized that her children were her greatest assets, that she need not feel ashamed of living her life for them, but could actually take pride in it.

In our society, if a woman is obsessed with her career, she is respected; if she is infatuated with her lover, she is envied; but should she manifest these same sentiments toward her children, she is immediately labeled "neurotic." This, despite the fact that there is no relationship so fulfilling as that of parent and child.

We can succeed in almost every area of life, but should we fail with our children, all our other accomplishments fade and we are left with the taste of ashes in our mouths. Yet our culture only grudgingly acknowledges the centrality of family.

Undoubtedly, there were many factors which contributed

to the undoing of Walter, but one thing was obvious: His personality was most certainly affected by our value system. In Walter's world, independence was a sign of masculinity which could be achieved only through succeeding financially. He was determined to make it big, and had no scruples about how he would do it.

As a matter of fact, it took him a long time to understand what he had done wrong outside of getting caught. Delores, he felt, should never have turned on him. As far as he was concerned, he was an exemplary husband, having provided her with everything a woman could want. And if he had someone else on the side, so what? Most of the guys he knew did the same. Walter did not recognize any authority beyond his own judgment. G-d to him was an abstract, and His Commandments had no bearing on his life. He prided himself on being self-made. To have turned to G-d, to have begged for His mercy, would have been a concession of weakness, and that was not part of his scene.

In our correspondence with Walter, we bared the phoniness of these pretensions and defined for him what our tradition teaches us about manhood. In Judaism, the man of stature is the one who has the strength of character to admit that he was wrong, that he must start anew and summon the courage to rise after having fallen. We cited the example of the mightiest man in history, the man who defeated Goliath singlehandedly, the man whose valorous deeds have been inscribed for all time in the annals of mankind: David, King of Israel, the true model of Jewish manhood.

The greatness of David was not to be found in his prowess on the battlefield, but in his psalms, which reflected the anguish in a man's heart and his total dependence on G-d. It is not the warrior David who was immortalized, but David the "sweet singer of Israel," who unashamedly cried out in the stillness of the night:

Have mercy on me and receive my supplication O
L-rd ...
Rebuke me not in Thy anger ...
My bed is drenched with my tears, my couch melts with
my weeping.

(Psalm 6:2, 7)

Indeed, there is no might, no discipline, to equal such
strength. But in a society in which emotions have to be subli-
mated, in which honesty is equated with simplemindedness,
man dare not admit to weakness. It's not only Delores and
Walter who encountered this problem; in a sense, all of us
are vulnerable. We cannot concede our deficiencies lest we
be found out, and therefore the road to repentence eludes us.

Our tenuous family ties further compound our loneliness
and deny us the incentive to reach beyond ourselves. Only
the pride of loved ones can make things worthwhile and
inspire us to try harder. But where such feelings are missing,
despondency sets in, and we wonder what it's all about. Our
accomplishments, our assets, even our thoughts and feelings,
assume significance only as they affect others. No matter how
many credits we have to our names, no matter how large a
fortune we amass, if we have no one to share it with, it all
becomes pointless.

At the outset of my career, as I became more and more
involved in public speaking, a little-known Yiddish language
publication would run stories on my appearances. My
beloved grandfather on my mother's side, Rabbi Tzvi Hirsch
Kohn (who survived the war and came to the U.S. in 1947),
was an avid reader of that daily. Every time a story appeared
about me, he would call, *"Esterl, mein kind,* Esther, my
sweet child, it's truly amazing what you have accomplished.
G-d watch over you always."

Those few words of my *zeide* meant more to me than any

accolade. The paper was of no special significance, and its circulation was negligible, yet to me it was the single most important coverage and I wouldn't have traded it for even a feature article in *The New York Times*.

Some time after *zeide* passed away, I lectured in Columbus, Ohio. While chatting with the local rabbi in his study, I noticed *zeide's* favorite paper lying on his desk. Catching my glance, the rabbi said: "There's a nice story about you in there."

But it was no longer important. My *zeide* was no longer here to take pride.

A man can fulfill his greatest aspirations and be accorded the highest honor, but if he is alone, if he has no family to rejoice in his triumphs, he will be left feeling empty and his achievements will be hollow. Be it joy, sorrow, or just everyday events, every man must feel that someone has a stake in his life, that someone cares and is concerned for him.

During the summer months, I usually lecture at a resort. On one of these occasions, my husband called to tell me that he had to officiate at a wedding and would be coming late. He insisted that I not wait up for him, since he had no way of knowing exactly when he would arrive.

Taking his advice, I quickly fell asleep, but awoke with a fright to a thunderstorm. I looked at my watch. It was 5:50 A.M. My husband had still not arrived. My heart started to pound. All sorts of horrible thoughts came to my mind. I called our home on Long Island as well as our synagogue, but there was no answer at either place. I started to panic. What if, G-d forbid, he had had an accident? I called the police for a road check, but there was nothing that they could tell me.

There I was, on the verge of hysteria, fighting back tears, praying to G-d that he arrive safely. At around 7:00 A.M. my phone finally rang. My husband, his voice tense with exhaustion, told me that the roads had flooded, his car had gotten stuck, and this was the first opportunity he had to get to a phone.

I closed my eyes and whispered, "Thank You, G-d."

At breakfast, I related the night's events to our table companion, a man in his early forties, highly successful in his profession and very popular among the guests at the hotel. His reaction was very odd. My story seemed to upset him. His face fell and his eyes darkened.

"You are a very lucky man, Rabbi," he said, turning to my husband. "If I were to drop dead today, believe me, no one would give a damn, no one would even know."

"Oh, come on," I protested, "how can you say such a thing?"

"I'm quite serious," he insisted calmly. "If I didn't return home one night, no one would care. After a while, perhaps someone would miss me, and they might even say, 'What a shame,' but I can assure you, their lives would continue just the same."

Slowly, the painful reality of his words sunk in. The man may have been affluent, he may have had everything going for him, but it was all pointless. He had no family, his life was empty. And yet, we continue to glorify the independent lifestyle. We advise our young people to put off marrying and having children. We warn them to have their fun while they can, because once the kids come, it will all be over.

I remember a reporter once telling me that he regretted that no one had ever bothered to tell him how much more fun it was to hold a baby in his arms than to go skiing.

At first I thought he was putting me on, but he was serious. He had put off having a family because he had been led to believe that children were parasites who were more of a burden than a source of joy.

If today we are encountering zero population growth, if child abuse is on the rise, if elderly parents are being abandoned, if young people opt to shack up and exploit one another rather than live by lasting commitment, it is because we have renounced family responsibility in order to better concentrate on ourselves. Herein lies our undoing. We have become so detached that we stand alone, so isolated that we can no longer make contact. In one of my letters, I explained this to Walter through an allegory.

Once upon a time, I wrote, there was a tree which stood majestically in the forest. Attached to one of its many branches was a leaf. But the leaf was not happy. Enviously, it watched the birds flying off to new worlds and experiences. "Ah," it mused, "if only I could shake off that branch which ties me to this tree."

One day, the leaf was granted its wish. A strong wind tore it from its branch and it joyfully tasted freedom. But its happiness was short lived. The leaf soon floated to the earth where it was trampled upon and ground into dust.

Poor leaf. It did not understand that once torn from its parent tree, it would not survive; once severed from its life-giving roots, it could not go on.

Every man is a leaf on a tree. When attached to his family, to his people, to his G-d, he lives and thrives. But the moment he cuts himself off and declares himself a free and independent being, he also detaches himself from the source of his blessing and renders himself vulnerable to loneliness and neuroses.

Those who suffer from this loneliness will not only try to drown their fear in alcohol, drugs, and phony gaiety, but will even feign illness in a desperate attempt to elicit sympathy. Their preoccupation with health, their constant running to doctors, and their general state of hypochondria, can often be directly traced to this need.

Evelyn Black was a very sick woman who lived on pills and needed constant medical attention. One of our members told me about her, and I went to visit her.

The maid who answered the door informed me that Mrs.

Black was resting. "But why don't you have a seat," she suggested, "and I will ask the nurse if she can see you."

I made myself comfortable, and as I admired the luxurious home, my heart went out to this unfortunate woman who, to all appearances, had everything to live for, yet could not enjoy it.

Soon the maid returned and told me that I could go in. The blinds in the bedroom were drawn and a nurse hovered over the huge bed.

"Thank you so much for coming," Evelyn said feebly.

She was an attractive woman in her late forties. Her coiffed red hair and manicured nails testified that, despite her condition, she was well cared for.

Evelyn told me of her many bouts with illness as well as her many frustrations. It soon emerged that in addition to her health problems, she was terribly lonely. Her husband, who was a senior partner in a law firm, was hardly ever home, and her two boys lived on the West Coast. She was dependent for all her needs on the nurse, whose arrogant manner conveyed just that. I visited Evelyn as often as I could, and a fast friendship developed between us.

Then, one day, we had a crisis in our *Hineni* organization. Two girls, whom we had just taken out of a cult, needed care and lodging. I thought of Evelyn's beautiful, empty home and decided to take a chance and ask her.

"Evelyn," I begged, "you must help us, even if only for a few days."

But Evelyn was reluctant. She assured me that there was nothing that she would have liked better, but her illness prevented her from doing so. After several days had gone by, however, and I still could not locate a place for the kids, she offered to give it a try.

Overnight, a miracle occurred. Instead of staying in bed, Evelyn made an effort to get up in the morning and supervise breakfast for the girls. She planned their day's schedule and discussed their problems. Soon she got rid of her nurse and began to take care of her own needs. By the time the kids were ready to leave, Evelyn had become a new person, involving herself in many of our organizational activities.

Now, Evelyn's illness was not a figment of her imagination. She was, and unfortunately still is, ill. Loneliness however, intensified her pain and made her a victim of her infirmity. But once she was given a sense of purpose and had someone to care for, she summoned the strength to fight and overcome her debility.

What emerges here is that loneliness is illness-conducive, while a strong family life infuses you with the will to fight.

I never heard either of my parents complain of illness or suffering, although over the years they have both been in and out of hospitals. But on each occasion, they managed to reach beyond their sick beds and overcome their illnesses.

Whenever I would visit the hospital, they would always assure me that everything was well, that there was no need for me to have come, and that I should go home and take care of my children. Their love for us was of such intensity that it actually enabled them to sublimate their pain so that we, their children, might be spared.

It was this total dedication to family that enabled my own Tante to retain her remarkable sense of humor throughout her difficult and tragic life. Tante had been widowed at an early age and lost a son only a few days prior to his Bar Mitzva, but her ability to laugh never left her. She dreaded the thought of becoming a burden, and to her dying day refused to give up her apartment and move in with her children. Even toward the end, when almost daily she would be rushed to the hospital for treatment, she always insisted on returning to her own home where she would courageously continue to fight against the debilitating disease that had taken hold of her life.

Tante found a measure of comfort in the knowledge that

her illness did not inhibit those whom she loved from going about their own lives. The very thought that she might be a burden to the family would have made her pain that much more unbearable.

The reverse, of course, was also true. We, the members of her family, never resented the responsibility of caring for her, and despite her protestations, never left her alone. Toward the end, Tante deteriorated rapidly. Her once strong, buxom body became frail and emaciated, but her laughter remained constant, and a visit to her remained a very special treat. On one of these occasions, I found it difficult to carry on a normal conversation. Her enfeebled state was just too painful to behold. Tante must have sensed my distress, because she immediately started to joke.

"There is nothing to be frightened of," she laughed. "The way I look, even the *Malach Hamoves*, the Angel of Death, would not want me." With that, she proceeded to entertain me with one of her myriad stories.

"Did I ever tell you about Moishe the *Melamed*, the Hebrew school teacher in our village? Well," she related, "he was a real *schlimazel*, a hard luck character, who was not only poor, but was always getting himself into trouble. One day, he fell gravely ill, and the news quickly spread that Moishe the *Melamed* was dying. Of course everyone felt very sorry, and as is usual in such cases, their sympathy was tinged with some guilt. They all came to visit, and brought him his favorite dish—goose liver fried in onions. Poor Moishe started to moan.

" 'Oy, oy,' he cried, 'what a bitter fate I have. Here is my favorite dish, goose liver, and I can't even eat it. When I was healthy, I could never have afforded it, but now, when I'm ready to die and I can no longer eat, they bring me goose liver. Oy, I have no *mazel*.'

"As the people kept coming, his frustration became even more maddening.

" 'There was a time when I would have enjoyed company,' he wailed, 'but then no one ever bothered to visit me. And now, when I want only a little peace and quiet, they keep banging on my door. Woe is me. When I wanted to live, they didn't let me live, and now, when I'm ready to die, they don't let me die!'

"You think that such stories can only occur to a *schlimazel* in the *shtetl?*" Tante asked laughingly. "Well, I tell you, things haven't changed all that much. What the people did to Moishe, the doctors tried to do to me.

"When I was healthy and could have enjoyed food, they kept yelling, 'You must diet!' And now, when I can't swallow, they keep stuffing me. When I had the strength to do things, they kept telling me to slow down. And now, when I can't even lift my head, they tell me to exercise. The old *melamed* was right. *They don't let you live, and they don't let you die.*

"I never forgot Moishe the *Melamed*," Tante laughed. "You needn't feel sorry for me. I lived a full life. I have no regrets, and if G-d should call me, I'm ready."

Tante's love for us prevented her from self-commiseration, from giving in to depression and irritability. She triumphed over her disease-racked body and bequeathed to us a legacy of love and laughter.

Whenever I look back on those childhood years, I always feel kind of sorry for today's children who are denied such rich family experiences, who are raised in the isolation of independent nuclear families and are never given the opportunity to participate in the lively, warm gatherings of grandparents, aunts, uncles, cousins, and distant relations, all united by a common bond called *mishpocha*.

But even as I write these lines, I am aware that skeptics will argue that the family life I described is contingent upon charismatic personalities such as Tante or my parents, and they are one of a kind, impossible to duplicate. What they ignore is that Tantes are not born in vacuums. It is families who give life to them, and every family can create its own colorful personalities. Families are self-generating, and in every generation G-d grants every *mishpocha* at least one "strong one," who assumes the responsibility of keeping everyone united.

As a case in point, a few days before Tante died, she called my mother in and officially appointed her to carry on.

"Maryam," she announced, "I leave everything to you. You will have to keep things going when I'm no longer here. The big borsht pot that I used for *Pesach* is yours. Make sure that you prepare the borsht in time and that there is enough to go around. Be certain that all those who received borsht from me will continue to get their jars. Now all the other extra large pots, plus my rolling pin, I leave to you, Maryam."

Having thus disposed of her most precious earthly possessions, Tante felt prepared to face her Creator. To this day, my mother, Tante's heir, prepares the jars of borsht for Passover. Not only do those people who were on Tante's list get their share, but my mother keeps adding her own new names. The family goes on.

You may still ask, if indeed the Tante types are the natural by-product of family life, why have so few families produced them?

While there are many contributory factors to the eclipse of the extended family, the most cogent one appears to be increased mobility. There is no getting away from it. The contemporary family is on the move. Whether it be for professional or socio-economic reasons, the fact remains that the family no longer stays put. Years ago, relatives lived within close proximity to one another, allowing for frequent visits and close ties. As a matter of fact, it was not unusual for three generations to live under one roof. Undoubtedly, such set-ups presented their own problems, but nevertheless, these conflicts were secondary to the sense of stability and warmth which the extended family afforded.

Nowadays, such familial underpinnings are missing. Tantes, *zeides*, and *bubbas* have become obsolete, and left on their own, the nuclear family finds it more and more difficult to remain united. Even as a tree that does not have deep roots is easily uprooted, so a family that does not have antecedents, that is not planted in its own rich soil, will be quickly blown away.

If *bubbas* and *zeides* are to enrich the lives of their children, they cannot be museum pieces who are seen only on formal occasions, at weddings or Bar Mitzvas. Families can reach out to one another only if they have someone real to reach out to. Such relationships cannot be sustained through long distance calls or recorded messages, but must be continuous and personal.

Only in our independence-oriented society can it happen that a bride studying her guest list will not recognize the names of her *mishpocha*, that cousins will meet for the first time at funerals, and that relatives will not know of each other's whereabouts. If our children are to be bequeathed a legacy of family life, if they are to have roots and strength of character, then relatives will have to be more than photos in an album.

"Who am I? What am I? Where did I come from?" are questions troubling the Kevins of our generation. They have no memories to sustain them, no *bubbas* or *zeides* to recall. And so, if the family is to survive intact, we will have to reconsider our priorities and carefully weigh the advisability of constantly uprooting ourselves. Mobility exacts a terrible penalty, which even the new job with its higher standard of living does not always justify.

To many, my outlook may appear unrealistic. After all, who in his right mind would forgo a higher income just to be near mom and dad? But let us consider: Is it really so foolish to renounce an increase in salary in order to see grandma and grandpa regularly? In the final analysis, what are the things in life that count, that are lasting and memorable?

Again, those of you who never experienced the warmth and love that only grandparents can convey will wonder what all the fuss is about. For you, it may be comparatively easy to give up family, because you never had one. But those who had the good fortune to grow up in the midst of loving aunts, uncles, and grandparents will forever cherish those childhood days, and will rightfully feel sorry for children who were denied such recollections.

I vividly recall when, a few months following my own marriage, my husband was offered a very prestigious rabbinic position in Miami, Florida. At that time, my husband was the spiritual leader of a modest congregation in Paterson, New Jersey, and the Florida pulpit seemed like a dream come true. Yet we decided to turn it down. As far as we were concerned, nothing could compensate for the separation that such a move would impose. To see our parents once or twice a year was simply not the way of life that we sought for ourselves or our children.

This is not to condemn those who have no options. There are always exceptional cases of couples who are compelled to take up residence in faraway places. Rather, my plea is directed to those who could be more discriminating were it not for their distorted values which associate family living with neuroses.

Yes, every one of us is a leaf on a tree. When attached to our family, to our people, to our G-d, we live and thrive. But the moment we cut ourselves off, we also detach ourselves from that source of blessing which renders our lives worthwhile.

seven

🐦

TO BE A WOMAN,
TO BE A MOTHER

YEARS AGO, a girl's role was clear cut. Practically from the moment of birth, parents planned her wedding, and she, in turn, grew up dreaming of the boy she would marry.

Today parents still wish for their daughters to marry and have families, but they are equally anxious for them to have careers. No longer do girls go to college simply to meet the right man. Today they take their education seriously, and are determined not only to graduate, but to pursue a profession as well. A new world has opened up for the contemporary female, yet instead of rejoicing in her newfound freedom, the variety of tempting choices she faces is literally tearing her apart.

Which way should she go? What should her role be?

Should she opt for marriage and children, she will feel that she has betrayed her education. Should she decide on a career, she will be overcome by feelings of guilt. There is only one thing of which she can be certain, and that is that she is bound to feel conflict. Indeed, how can it be otherwise? In a society where status is commensurate with personal achievement, and where work is evaluated by its financial return, why should anyone devote day and night to an unpaid task, motherhood?

133

It appears that to be a female today is to be consigned to a schizophrenic existence. On the one hand, the pressure is on to be loving, self-sacrificing mothers; on the other, we downgrade the importance of parenting.

Laurie Braverman had been one of my brighter students, and when she called to say that she would like to come over, I anticipated her visit with pleasure. I hadn't seen Laurie for at least eight years, and I was anxious to find out how she was doing.

"Well, Laurie, given your talent and drive, I bet you're a doctor already," I said half-jokingly as I greeted her.

I was more correct than I realized. Laurie was just finishing up her residency and was engaged to be married to a fellow physician. We had a long chat as we tried to catch up on the past eight years.

"Rebbetzin, I have a serious problem," she confided. "You must help me."

For the life of me, I couldn't imagine what could be bothering Laurie. She seemed to have everything that a girl could want, a brilliant career, love, looks, and money. What else was there?

As if sensing my bewilderment, she interrupted my thoughts. "I'll bet you can't imagine what I have on my mind," she continued. "I really don't know where to start, but maybe the best way would be for me to tell you that in six weeks, Jeff and I will be married."

Laurie hesitated for a moment. "Please don't laugh at me. Jeff thinks I'm crazy for worrying about these things, but I have always been an organized person, and I like to plan things out."

"Laurie," I said, reaching out for her hand, "you know that I would never laugh at anything you had to say. Just tell me what it's all about."

She nodded, took a deep breath, and came to the point.

"I want to have a family, Rebbetzin, I love children. As a matter of fact, I probably wouldn't mind having half a dozen."

"Well that's great! What's the problem then?"

"That's what Jeff says, but there *is* a problem, and I can't ignore it any longer. Rebbetzin, I've come a long way. I worked very hard to become a doctor. I love it, and I cannot give it up to become a housewife."

"Oh, come on, Laurie," I tried to reason with her. "Why should you worry about these things now? You're not even married. I'm sure you'll find a way to manage, and everything will work out."

"But that's exactly it," she said. "Nobody worries about having babies. They just have them. Well, I can't be that way, Rebbetzin. I grew up in a home where there was always a maid taking care of us. My mother was hardly ever there, and I swore that when I had children I would be different. Well, here I am, and I'll probably end up being worse than my mother ever was."

I tried to reassure her, but the more I tried to calm her, the more tense she became.

"Rebbetzin, I'm going to tell you something that I never told anyone. Every winter, my parents would go off someplace. Well, one year, I must have been around twelve, our maid quit two days before they were to leave. You can't imagine how upset my mother and father were. Finally, a neighbor found us a new girl and my parents were able to go off on schedule. But before they left, my mother made a big fuss about locking up all her valuables. 'You can never trust a new maid,' she told us again and again, and yet it never occurred to her that she was entrusting *us*, her children, to that new maid! It's been many years, Rebbetzin, but that scene always stayed with me. I've never gotten over it."

Laurie's story left me nonplussed. How many other children, I wondered, have been left scarred by our mixed-up priorities? How can we undo the damage?

"Oh, I've thought it all out," she went on. "I do have another option. I don't *have* to work. Jeff can support me in style. But, Rebbetzin, I would go crazy. I love my profession and I could never give it up. I remember you telling us in your class that if we have a problem, we should look for the solution in the Bible. Okay, Rebbetzin, I have a problem. What do I do?"

Laurie's conflict was real. What should a woman's priority be?

Of all the heroines of the Bible, I thought that Laurie could best identify with Rachel. She, too, was blessed with everything that a woman could dream of—beauty, wealth, prestige, a loving husband, and even a career. Yet it is written that Rachel cried out in agony, "Give me a child lest I die!" (*Genesis* 30:1).

"Well, Laurie," I said, "it seems that the Bible teaches us that no matter what you achieve, you will never feel quite fulfilled if you do not have a baby in your arms."

As we studied further, Laurie discovered that Rachel was not the exception, but the rule. All the great women of the Bible reaffirmed her plea, and most significantly, G-d Himself deferred to it. In promulgating His Commandments, He exempted women from observing those rituals that were limited to a specific day, time, or season, so that nothing would interfere with the proper nurturing of children. Rather than see little ones forsaken, G-d preferred that women absent themselves from synagogue and forgo praying with a quorum, for the raising of children is, in itself, the highest form of Divine service.

Once we established these priorities, we delved further and tried to determine whether it was possible to combine career and homemaking, whether there was any precedent for it in the Bible. I had Laurie study the life of the matriarch Sarah, and she discovered that in addition to her being the first Jewish mother, she was also a career wife. Sarah was a full fledged partner to her husband in teaching and disseminating the Word of G-d, yet there is no evidence that she ever experienced tension between home and career. It soon emerged that Sarah lived with priorities and never confused her profession with the needs of her children. Her dedication to teaching and her loyalty to family occupied unique places in her life, but her home always came first. She built her career around her child rather than the child around the career.

I told Laurie that I myself had followed this teaching. Although I was always involved in some sort of career, I never lost sight of my priorities. For example, when the children were small, I tried to do my work at home. The classes which Laurie attended were held in my kitchen or den. As the children became older, I allowed myself more latitude, but I always kept my priorities in sight. My trips abroad were always scheduled during the summer months, when the children were away at camp. And when I traveled in the United States, I always returned home the same day, even if this meant that I had to catch a midnight flight. To this day, I refuse invitations that would take me away from my family on the Sabbath or holidays. Those occasions are simply too precious, and I would never give them up.

"It's not a matter of having to renounce your career," I told Laurie, "but rather, it's a question of priorities. If you had listened to your own words, you would have realized that what hurt you the most was that in your home these priorities were never clearly defined, that it appeared as if possessions and good times were more important to your mother than you were. Had your mother been obliged to work, chances are you could have identified with her efforts, and even volunteered to pitch in and help, but what really troubled you was the nagging suspicion that you came second in her life."

It was her mother's obsession with self to the exclusion of everything else that left Laurie resentful and bitter, and it was against this that I cautioned her to be on guard.

"If you raise your children with the knowledge that they are the most important part of your life, then they will feel secure and confident in your love," I told Laurie. "It is only where children sense that they are at the bottom of the pecking order that they feel betrayed and neglected."

It was to embed this priority of children into our psyches that the Almighty, in His infinite wisdom, denied to Jewish mothers that which he gave so freely to others. It wasn't only Rachel who cried out in anguish, "Give me a child, lest I die!" All the mothers of our people went through the same agonizing experience: Sarah, Rebecca, Chana—G-d denied them all. He made them suffer, plead, pray, and shed tears, and only then did He grant them the gift of children. It was as if G-d wished to insure that we never take the blessing of children for granted, as if He wished for us to be more devoted and committed than is normal. And so, we became obsessed with motherhood, but this obsession gave life to generations of prophets and scholars, sons and daughters who devoted themselves to the service of mankind, and I told Laurie that she could follow in their footsteps with pride.

Laurie, however, had to wrestle not only with her own personal conflicts, but with the insidious influence of her culture as well. In her circle, to be a devoted mother was not only regarded as a parasitic experience, but worse, mothers were accused of emasculating their sons and provoking neuroses (Philip Roth's *Portnoy's Complaint* and Philip Wylie's *Generation of Vipers* were in no small measure responsible for creating this warped image).

While all women have suffered from such defamation, Laurie was more affected by it than others, for it is the Jewish mother who was most vilified. It is she who was stereotyped as neurotically overprotective and jealously domineering.

"Don't be taken in by psychological jargon," I told Laurie. "Strip away the words and define for yourself just what this Jewish neurosis is supposed to imply. Does it mean that instead of running off to play tennis, a mother worries that her children are properly cared for, that they eat and sleep well, and yes, that they get their Jewish penicillin, chicken soup?

"Does it mean that a mother worries that her children come home safely when they are out at night, that they put on their coats when it's bitter cold, and, as they get older, that they find good husbands and wives? Is this why the Jewish mother is labeled neurotic?"

And so, I told Laurie never to be apologetic about her devotion to her children, or to feel insecure about being a Jewish mother, for if anyone has some explaining to do, it is those mothers who shirk their responsibility by rationalizing that youngsters have to be made strong and self-reliant, who, in their selfishness, remain deaf and blind to the cries of their troubled children, who run off to distant places, abandoning their youngsters to the care of strangers. It is they who have to apologize, for the harm that they have inflicted will be felt for generations and generations to come.

To be a Jewish mother is not only to give birth to a child, but it is to join G-d in partnership, establish links to the future, and bring blessing to the world. Therefore, our sages, when referring to the Hebrew word for children, proclaimed, "Read not *'boniach,'* your children, but *'baniach,'* your builders, for children are the true builders of the world" (*Talmud Berakhot* 64a).

Chana, the exquisite woman of the Bible, was the one

who gave expression to this ideal. For many years, she could not bear children, and wept unremittingly that G-d might take pity on her.

> Why weepest thou?
> Why eatest thou not?
> And why is thy heart grieved?
> Am I not better to you than ten sons, her husband asked?
> (*Samuel* 1:8)

But Chana could not be consoled, and she made a vow: "If Thou will give me a child, Oh G-d, I will raise him for You all the days of his life."

Chana was granted her wish, and she raised a son who became Samuel the Prophet. Thus she paved the immortal road from the cradle to the great academies of Torah, where to this very day children are trained to become *builders of peace*. This is the essence of being a Jewish woman and mother.

The legacy has been bequeathed. Laurie has only to possess it. True, the conflicts remain; they are an integral part of twentieth-century culture. But those who have the wisdom to follow the course charted by their ancestors will never stumble.

It is not only career women like Laurie who must bear these priorities in mind. Housewives who pride themselves on the amount of time that they invest in their children must also understand what mothering is all about. If children are to become "builders of peace," then no limit can be set on the love of their mothers, and it is this priority that must always be kept in mind.

My own mother defined it most beautifully when she conducted a seminar on traditional Jewish cuisine for our *Hineni* movement. To give a little background: Mama is not what you would call a homebody. She was, and continues to be, an activist if there ever was one. In war as in peace, mama has always been involved. From rescue missions in Hungary to teaching school in New York, to keeping the synagogue organized, she never hesitated to take on a job. But when someone suggested that my mother conduct a cooking class, it was no small matter for me to get her to agree.

Like all *Yiddishe* mamas, she has no written recipes, but is of the school that measures "a little bit of this, a little bit of that." Worse still, she can't understand how any woman can fail to know how to cook. All girls are supposed to grow up with that ability. Finally, after much persuasion, she acceded, and since her reputation was well established, her class was anticipated with much excitement. The women all came prepared with notebooks and tape recorders.

"Ladies," my mother began, "I must warn you that cooking takes a lot of time, so my advice to you is, instead of *patchkening*, messing around in the kitchen, take care of your children. More than home-baked cookies, they need love."

And with that introduction, mama took out the pots and pans. "Now I'll give you recipes," she said, "but the only recipes that are worthwhile are the ones that will make *Shabbos* and *Yomtov* more meaningful to your family."

For a moment, the ladies were taken aback by my mother's bluntness, but as they started to make *Shabbos* kugel and gefilte fish, they also gained renewed respect for this little woman, their teacher. They may have come for a cooking class, but they learned something far more precious—priorities. The raising of children takes priority over all else. That is the essence of the Jewish woman.

eight

TO BE A MAN, TO BE A FATHER

EVEN AS BEING A WOMAN today entails conflict, so being a man in twentieth-century society means coping with constant stress. The pressure is on to make it to the top, to achieve, and to succeed. As a result, men not only have shorter life expectancies than women, but they also succumb to coronaries, ulcers, and nervous breakdowns faster than their female counterparts. What is rather remarkable about all this is that, despite modern man's concern with well-being, health, and longevity, he does not rebel and free himself from the burdens which sap his vitality and deprive him of his very life.

Harold was a friend of ours. He was only in his early forties when he suddenly passed away, leaving a wife and two children. He had been a good man who lived solely for his family, which in our culture means that he saw to their every need and shielded them from worry.

Harold's troubles started when the unions got on his back. He couldn't make ends meet and fell deeper and deeper into debt. His accountant advised him to remortgage his business, but the banks denied his application. Harold felt trapped. One night, he woke his wife; he had sharp pains in his chest. By the time she got him to the hospital, it was too late. He was dead.

143

Harold's story is typical. It is the story of millions of Americans who literally fall apart the minute they hit bottom.

As a teenager, I remember studying about the great stock market crash of 1929 and the difficulty I had understanding it. How, I wondered, could adult men, fathers of children, leap from windows just because they had lost their money? Did they really think that they meant so little to their families that if they could no longer provide, they wouldn't be wanted?

"You don't understand," my social studies teacher told me. "You are young. You never experienced the horror of losing everything."

I smiled to myself. The teacher wasn't fully aware of my background. I told him of the time when we were deported, forced to abandon our home and all our earthly possessions. The Nazis awakened us from our sleep, gave us a few minutes to get ready, and threw us out into the night. Terrified, we stood on the street, and I held on for dear life to the only thing I was able to take with me, my favorite doll.

Our gentile neighbors came to gawk and to ransack our home. Among them I spotted my little friend, Marta. She was our superintendent's daughter, and for as long as I could recall, we had always played together. She stood there with her father, and she must have seen me, because suddenly, she made her way toward me. Marta was coming to say good-bye, I thought.

But as Marta came close, she grabbed for my doll.

"My father said I can take whatever I want," she sneered. "You can't keep anything."

"Give me back my doll," I cried. "It's mine, it's mine!"

Marta and her father just stood there laughing.

"It seems you haven't learned the facts of life yet," her father taunted. "You're a dirty Jew, see, and where you're going, you won't need toys."

With that, he opened his toothless mouth and spat.

"But don't worry," he continued, "Marta here will take care of all your things, won't you, Marta?" he said, patting her on the head and still laughing.

Yes, I knew what it felt like to be stripped of all earthly possessions. True, I was only a child, and true, that doll was only a toy, but to me it represented all my holdings. Yet somehow I understood that a doll was just a doll, and not the sum total of my existence, and the adults among us understood it even better. Throughout that long nightmare, I cannot recall even one instance in which a man committed suicide because his possessions were taken from him. And when I think of those years of darkness and contrast them to today, I feel a certain sadness for those whose lives are so barren, whose faith is so thin, that under financial stress they have no recourse but to fall apart.

There is nothing new about man being under pressure. From time immemorial, he had to sacrifice to earn a livelihood. "By the sweat of your brow shall you eat bread" (*Genesis* 3:19) is the curse with which man was banished from the Garden of Eden, and which pursues him to this very day. And yet there is something different about our modern day oppression, something so totally destructive that very few survive it intact.

To be a success today is to be out there in the jungle where it's dog eat dog, where in order to survive, a man has to be ruthless, cutthroat, and callous. Out there, it's not what a man is, but what he has that counts. He dare not show his feelings or exhibit tenderness lest he be accused of being weak or effeminate. Although of late there has been some movement in this area, nevertheless, in most circles, a man's conversation is generally limited to "man talk." Business, sports, cars, and sexual exploits are acceptable; anything else is a contradiction of that macho image.

This image of manhood is at the root of the contemporary

male's problem. Even as Philip Roth vilified the Jewish mother, so authors like Hemingway brutalized the American male. It was Papa Hemingway who held up the bullfight, the battlefield, and the exploitation of woman as the true symbols of macho. Hemingway protagonists (and by extension, the ideal male) are strong, rugged types who deny their feelings and cannot express compassion or warmth. They are supermen who are not allowed to admit to their fears or succumb to tears, not even in prayer to the Almighty.

This macho image, which thrives on the external and superficial, was at the root of Harold's undoing. No sooner did he lose his assets than he crumbled. In contrast, in Jewish life, a man's prestige is commensurate with his knowledge of Torah, his compassion, his charitable deeds, and his self-discipline—qualities which are internalized and not subject to the winds of change. A man who has such inner strength, no matter where life may take him, no matter what problems he may encounter, will always be able to overcome, for no one will be able to deprive him of his manhood. It comes from within his soul.

As a young girl, I spent a year studying and teaching in Jerusalem. Early one morning on my way to class, I chanced upon an old Yemenite street cleaner, who drew my attention because he seemed to be talking to himself. As I came closer and his words became audible, I realized that he was reciting intricate passages from the Talmud. Later I found out that in Yemen, this same man had been a rabbi, but having no means of support in his new country, he cheerfully took to cleaning the streets of Jerusalem. He may have been sweeping the gutter, but his heart and mind were anchored to ideals that propelled him into other worlds.

The old Yemenite Jew was following in the footsteps of the great ones of his people, Rabbi Yochanan the shoemaker, Hillel the water carrier, and others, men who never allowed their economic status to deprive them of their self-esteem,

for they associated manhood with the legacy of the patriarchs.

Torah, Bible; *avodah,* worship; and *gemilas chasidim,*
acts of loving kindness, were their distinguishing characteristics. These ideals were constantly held up as life goals, and
as early as the nursery, Jewish mothers implanted them in
the hearts of their infants:

> Run my son, run hard
> and enter the house of your teacher.
> Search and seek only in the Torah,
> For her wealth is better than rubies,
> Her rewards greater than all treasure.

These lullabies not only rocked the babies to sleep, but
accompanied them throughout life. The greatest compliment
that could have been given a Jewish man was to call him a
talmid chochem, a student of Divine wisdom. It is the Torah
that lent status to his life, made him a desirable candidate
for marriage, and accorded him respect in the community.

I remember the surge of pride I myself felt when told by
those who had been interned with my husband in the concentration camps that even under the most inhumane conditions, he would recite Talmudic passages that he had committed to memory. To me, there was no greater testimony to
his manhood than the realization that, despite starvation,
frostbite, lice, and beatings, the study of Torah remained his
supreme priority. This quest is so much a part of our people
that even today, in our sophisticated, high pressure society,
there are those who continue to live by its dictum.

Jerry Wollman was one of the founders of our organization. He was not only a successful attorney, but a remarkable
man in every sense. I had an appointment to see him one day
on some *Hineni* business, and I was surprised to be told that
he was in conference and could not be disturbed. But Jerry
must have heard my voice, because suddenly he appeared

and beckoned me right in. You can imagine my astonishment when I discovered that the "conference" his secretary was referring to was a session in Torah learning.

But I guess I needn't have been that shocked. After all, Jerry was a man who lived his Judaism, and the study of Torah is what Jewish manhood is all about.

It's all a matter of discipline and priorities. Once a man perceives that Torah learning can enrich his life and lend meaning to his days, there is nothing that can dissuade him from dedicating himself to it.

It was the patriarch Jacob who bequeathed this relentless yearning for G-d's Word, and throughout the millennia, our men have followed in his footsteps. When the Romans conquered the Holy Land, they forbade the study of Torah under pain of death. Undaunted, our people clandestinely continued to study. One of the Roman generals accosted Rabbi Akiva and asked, "How is it that you Jews are so spiteful and senseless? Don't you realize that we are onto your tricks, that we will catch you and burn you at the stake? What possible benefit can you have from studying that ancient nonsense?"

Rabbi Akiva looked at the pompous Roman and decided to answer him with an allegory.

"Once upon a time, there was a shrewd old fox who went to the seashore. He wanted to have fish for dinner, so he cleverly called out, 'Come out, save yourselves, fishermen are coming to catch you!'

"But the fish were onto the old fox's tricks. If we cannot survive in our own element, they reasoned, surely we will never make it on dry land.

"What water is to the fish, the Torah is to the Jew," Rabbi Akiva told the Roman. "True, our lives may be in jeopardy while we are studying, but if we abandon our Torah, we will cease to exist altogether."

This study of G-d's Book is not to be confused with scholarship or intellectual attainment. For the Jew, Torah study is his very life, the source of his existence. Today, as we experience a resurgence of Jewish commitment in these United States, Torah learning has become a priority for more and more of our men. The story of Jerry Wollman is not unusual. Today there are countless professionals, business people and students, who stop in the midst of a hectic day to enter the world of the spiritual. Today there are thousands upon thousands of young men, and their number is constantly increasing, who have happily renounced pragmatic career goals in order to dedicate their days and their nights to that sacred study of Torah.

In Israel, young men who study G-d's Holy Book are exempt from army service, for the government recognizes that even as soldiers are needed at the front, the spiritual army of the Jew must also be kept alive in the great halls of the academies.

My beloved grandfather, Rabbi Tzvi Hirsh Kohn, who was a descendent of Aaron, the High Priest, devoted his entire life to the study of Torah and the pursuit of peace. Whenever I would visit his modest apartment, I would find him seated at his table with his great books opened before him, studying.

In his last days, as illness ate away at his enfeebled body, his eyesight also dimmed, and the learning which he loved so passionately became increasingly difficult. Nevertheless, his books remained open. Lovingly, he would caress the pages, and as he did, he recalled from memory those passages that he was no longer able to read.

And then, one day, my mother called, "Come quickly, *zeide* is very sick."

My husband and I grabbed our four children and ran. By the time we arrived, our beloved *zeide* was semi-conscious. The room was full of people, but only quiet weeping was audible. One of my aunts chided me for bringing the children. "It's no place for little ones," she said. But I paid no heed, and made my way with them to *zeide*'s bedside.

"*Zeide*," I whispered, fighting to hold back the tears. "It is I, your granddaughter, Esther. I brought the children. Look, *zeide*, they are all here. Bless them, *zeide*, you are our *Kohen Gadol*, our High Priest. Please, *zeide*, bless them."

Slowly, my grandfather opened his eyes. His lips moved, but no sound came forth. He lifted his arm and beckoned to the children. His trembling hands covered each of their little heads in turn.

My *zeide* wished to speak again. I looked around for my father. If anyone could understand what my *zeide* was trying to say, it would be he. My father bent his head close to *zeide*'s lips, and when he straightened up, he wept. "*Zeide*," he told us, "wishes to be carried to the bookcase so that he might say farewell to his beloved life partners, the Holy Books of the Torah."

It happened more than ten years ago. My youngest son, Osher Anshil, was only four years old at the time, but he remembers it well, and today *zeide*'s books have become *his* best friends.

If only Harold had had Torah wisdom to sustain him, he could have admitted to his wife and children that he had problems and needed their help without feeling that his manhood was compromised. Had he lived by Torah values, he would have been revered for his knowledge, admired for his generosity, and loved for his kindness, rather than for his financial attainment. Had he only had that insight, he could have retained his self-worth even in face of financial disaster.

Avodah, worship, is the second legacy bequeathed to Jewish men by our forefathers. Isaac gave expression to it when he offered the ultimate prayer and placed himself on the altar of sacrifice for the greater glory of G-d.

How far modern man has come from this pure concept of prayer was first brought to my attention by my husband.

"In my home town of Gyongyos," he told me one day, "if a man failed to show up at synagogue, we knew something was wrong. But here, it's just the opposite. If I see a new face at services, I know there is trouble. Either someone is ill, dying, or undergoing a personal crisis, for why else would he come to pray?"

The more I thought about it, the more I realized that my husband was right. Prayer, which had once been the language of the strong, the powerful, and the wise, has, in our society, become the supplication of the beggar, the murmur of the sick, and the whimper of the troubled. You pray if you have a need, but if all is well, who needs G-d?

But that is not the legacy of Isaac. His prayer was not a petty enumeration of needs and wants. Isaac's service was an unconditional declaration of *"Hineni,* here I am, O G-d, ready to do your bidding, to fulfill Your every Commandment."

Three times daily, a man would enter the Divine Palace and stand in the presence of his King. No sooner would he arise, then he would envelop himself in his *tallis,* prayer shawl, and dedicate his heart, mind, and soul, to the service of the L-rd. Thus, he would go forth fortified, ready to confront the challenges that awaited him in that outside world.

Tefila, the Hebrew word for prayer, has no relation to requests or pleas. Rather, it is a means for inner appraisal and profound introspection.

"Where is your life at? What have you accomplished? What about your family, your people?" are all questions with which G-d challenges man in the moment of prayer. Prayer invites every man to bare his soul, to evaluate his life in the presence of the King of Kings, and that experience becomes what the Bible terms *avodah she b'lev,* the labor of the heart.

It happens almost magically. The heart which had been rendered callous is sensitized, humanized, and cleansed of all impurities, and the soul that has been wounded and hurt is healed.

Although prayer demands total self-judgment, when the descendents of Isaac stand in the presence of the King, all their prayers are phrased with *we* rather than *I*, for they perceive that it is in the greater *we* that their own happiness will be fulfilled, that by seeking blessing for the nation, their own blessing will be found. But if there is one request that they do have, it is that G-d may deem them worthy of service, of sanctifying His Holy Name, for there is no greater privilege to which a man can aspire than to be a trusted ambassador in the Royal Palace of the King of Kings.

Throughout the centuries, it was through these prayers that our people were able to overcome the atrocities inflicted upon them, and it was through these prayers that they were able to defy even death and triumph over their enemies.

A fellow survivor told me about the day when he was deported to Auschwitz. The Nazis had rounded up all his townspeople and marched them off to the railroad station. As the cattle cars pulled into the station, panic broke out. Children screaming, old people crying, men and women standing immobilized, frozen with fear.

Suddenly, a shot pierced the air. A young man fell dead.

"Yossele, Yossele, my son!" an old man wailed as he fell upon the bleeding boy.

But a Nazi soon prodded the old man with his rifle and kicked him into the cattle car in which my friend was already standing. The train started to roll. The air in the car became fetid, and as the meager supply of food and water were exhausted, despair took over.

Throughout this time, the old man kept mumbling to himself. His eyes were glazed and demented. He had obviously lost his sanity. My friend noticed that under his coat he was hiding a small canteen of water, which he seemed to be guarding with his life.

"Why don't you drink, you'll feel better," my friend tried to tell him. But the old man did not respond.

At last the train came to its final destination. The bellowing of orders, the barking of dogs, and the gunshots started all over again.

The old man, together with all the elderly, was placed on a line for the gas chambers. And it was only then that he opened his canteen.

Poor old man, my friend thought to himself. Now, before he dies, he will drink.

But the old man did not drink. Instead, he took the precious drops of water and carefully poured them over his hands, and as he did so, he whispered the mourners' *Kaddish: "Yisgadal, v'Yiskadash, Sh'mey Rabboh*, Magnified and Sanctified be Thy Holy Name."

The old man was a descendent of the patriarch Isaac. His washing of hands was the *akedah*. His *kaddish* was an echo of the royal plea of David, who despite personal persecution and suffering cried out, "One thing I ask of the L-rd, only one thing do I desire—to dwell in the house of the L-rd, all the days of my life" (*Psalm 27: 4*).

Obviously, not everyone is able to aspire to such lofty service. It is more honest for the great majority of us to admit that we pray for our own welfare and that of our families. But that, too, is positive, for if through our needs we are inspired to pray, from that initial contact with G-d, a total transformation can take place.

Had Harold been familiar with this power of prayer, his anxieties could have been converted into an expression of faith and his financial disaster could have served to bring him closer to his Creator. Thus, that which at first glance appeared destructive could ultimately have become his blessing.

Of all the attributes associated with Jewish manhood, it is the third concept, *gemilas chasadim,* loving kindness, that I find most difficult to communicate. Admittedly, Torah and worship are not easily explained either, but at least there is a context of scholarship and prayer through which they can be understood.

But there is no such association when it comes to loving kindness. If anything, limitless compassion is viewed in our society as weakness. It is not only Papa Hemingway who is responsible for this. The seeds of modern man's brutalization go very deep. We are the heirs to cultures where cruelty was worshipped and kindness was scorned, in which entertainment was to see a human being devoured by beasts, in which the weak and infirm were abandoned on mountaintops, in which a man could kill his wife and child with impunity, and in which chivalry was synonymous with bloodshed.

Although we pride ourselves on our sophistication and our cultural evolution, nothing much has changed beyond names and places. The arena has been replaced by the boxing ring, and we continue to cheer wildly while one man beats another to a pulp. Our T.V. heros are the tough and the ruthless, who can kill without a pang of conscience, and we admire those who crush and trample others on their way to success. Our streets are jungles, violence and sadism are rampant, and we tell our children that to survive they have to be tough and callous.

In this context, how can I explain the meaning of *gemilas chasadim,* loving kindness?

There are those who would suggest that in today's terminology loving kindness could best be illustrated through the concept of philanthropy. But here, too, we are sadly lacking, for if you were to have asked Harold, he would have told you that, indeed, he was very much involved in charitable causes, and yet he did not have the slightest notion of what loving kindness was all about. To be sure, he was a generous man, and had been honored by many organizations. But the moment Harold hit bottom, he also discovered that his charitable deeds mocked him and made his downfall that much more painful. Whereas in the past he had been consulted, sought after, and respected, overnight he became a nobody. He could no longer deliver, and as a result he was no longer important. Harold discovered the reality of American life. If you have money in your pocket, you can do no wrong; but the moment you lose it, you also lose your status.

The philanthropy which was supposed to make Harold a better person left him cynical and bitter. But the ramifications go much deeper, for if acts of charity are to render one a better person, then charity must be a giving and personal experience that transcends the mere writing of a check. Modern-day philanthropy, however, most often works in reverse, and fosters an attitude of arrogance and condescension.

And so the challenge still remains—how to explain loving kindness? Allow me to resort to that well-trodden Jewish way, a story.

It is told that two peasants once sat at an inn drinking.

"Tell me, do you love me?" one of them drunkenly asked his companion.

"Of course, I love you," the other replied, equally drunk.

"Well, then, if that be the case, tell me what is in my heart? What hurts me?"

The first peasant looked up in surprise. "How on earth should I know? You never told me."

"Ah," the second answered, "you are not really my friend. You don't really love me, because if you truly cared, you would have sensed my feelings without my having to tell you."

A Chassidic rabbi who overheard this exchange explained to his disciples that the peasant, in his simplicity, conveyed the essence of loving kindness: to perceive the feelings of another so totally that there is no need for explanations, to identify with his pain so completely that you can actually feel his heartache, and to share his happiness to the point of totally rejoicing with him.

Harry Berger was a prosperous businessman, the father of two lovely children, and he didn't seem to have a care in the world. Then, one day, I introduced him to my father, and for the first time, I saw Harry open up. He spoke about things he had never spoken of before.

"Rabbi," he whispered, his voice trembling, "I had a sweet, beautiful little girl. She was killed in a car accident."

My father clasped him in his arms, and with his tears soothed the sharpness of his pain.

"It's amazing," Harry said to me later. "Your father hardly knows me, and yet he cried for me."

"You are wrong Harry," I said. "My father does know you. He feels your pain more than you will ever know, for his heart is filled with loving kindness."

It was this feeling of loving kindness that infused my father with superhuman strength and enabled him to enter the jaws of the lion and bring hope and salvation to more than three thousand young men who were scheduled to be deported to the mines of Bor from our city of Szeged. It was this generosity of spirit that kept the doors of our home open, and it was this compassion that to this very day enables my father to embrace young people who have fallen prey to drugs, cults, and assimilation, and lovingly call them "my children."

Throughout the years, all sorts of people passed through our home, but there is one in particular who stands out in my mind. He was dressed in filthy rags and was so repulsive that we actually cringed at the sight of him. He had once been a boxer, but too many fights and poverty had disfigured him, and he became the subject of mockery in the neighborhood. My father couldn't bear to see his pain. He brought him home, sat him at our table, and taught him how to pray. The man had never been Bar Mitzvaed, but my father managed even that, and on the day that he was called up to the Torah, he wept like a baby. I doubt very much if ever there was a Bar Mitzva boy prouder than he.

As the old boxer became part of our daily *minyan*, the quorum required for prayer, his self-esteem grew, and what was once a wretched beggar, through the magic of loving kindness, became a man.

My father's name is Abraham, and he inherited his loving kindness from the patriarch himself. Father Abraham's influence has been so far-reaching, that to this very day, if someone is bereft of compassion, it is assumed that he cannot be of the patriarch's seed.

Abraham's love for his fellow man was so all-encompassing, that while he silently accepted the many trials and tribulations placed on his own shoulders, he could not bear to remain passive when confronted with the affliction of others. He felt their pain with such intensity that he even pleaded for the wicked men of Sodom. And when his nephew Lot was taken into captivity, he gathered the members of his household and went forth to battle armies and kings in order to save him. It never occurred to Abraham that he was jeopardizing his life and the life of his family for someone who might be undeserving, or might not repay in kind. There was only one motivation in his heart—loving kindness.

The tent of our father Abraham had an opening on every side, so that no matter from which direction a stranger might come, he would find a door open to him, bidding him welcome. But the love of Abraham was of such magnitude that he was not merely content to open his home, he actually went forth in search of the destitute. Tenderly, he would bring them home, nurse their wounds, and soothe their pain.

By present day standards, such commitment to humanity would be regarded as a sign of instability. No man in his right mind would fight for his enemies, bring beggars into his home, or endanger the lives of his own household in order to save strangers, and yet that is the legacy of loving kindness. From the patriarch Abraham to my own father, Abraham, our people have never departed from it.

Today, as the descendents of Abraham have returned to their ancient land, this heritage of compassion remains the dominant spirit which shapes their lives.

No sooner did they declare the State than they remembered those open doors of their father's tent. They sent forth the call to the young, to the old, to the insane, to the infirm, to the blind, to the lame, to the unwanted of the earth. To all of them they bid welcome. They were all wanted in the land of Abraham.

But the story did not end there. History repeats itself. Even as Abraham's nephew was taken into captivity, hostages were again taken. It was 1976. A French plane was hijacked. The lives of 143 people hung by a hair. The nations watched in horror, but no one reacted.

But the children of Abraham could not bear to remain silent. Remembering their father, they gathered their courage and rose up to the skies. Their planes soared over enemy territory, but no eye detected them, the radar did not pick them up.

The world was astounded. How did they do it?

Rationalizations were advanced, articles were written, books were published, but the truth remains hidden, the story has yet to be told. Indeed, how did they do it?

I have often thought about it, and I am convinced that our father Abraham, the man of loving kindness, who feels the pain of every soul, surely approached the Heavenly Throne.

"Almighty G-d," he must have pleaded, "let me accompany my sons on their way to Uganda."

And G-d, whose name is also Loving Kindness, could not deny His loyal servant, and sent him forth to give cover to those who were flying in the skies.

Operation Entebbe, the story of the soldiers of Israel, the children of Abraham, who, following in the footsteps of their father, responded in loving kindness to the desperate plea for help to which the rest of the world remained silent.

nine

ॐ

FATHERS AND CHILDREN

IT IS TOLD THAT when G-d was about to bestow the Torah upon the Jewish people, there was much consternation in the Heavens above.

"Almighty G-d," the angels pleaded, "You are about to give away Your most sacred treasure, the Torah, and yet what guarantees do You have for its safekeeping?"

G-d considered the words of the angels and found them to be just. But what can mere mortals offer the Creator of the universe? What guarantees can they possibly give?

There were those who counseled that the prophets, the sages, the rabbis, be held as surety. But G-d did not accept.

Then there were those who advised that the patriarchs, the matriarchs, the ancestors of the nation, act as guarantors, but still G-d did not accept.

Finally, someone suggested that the children, the little ones, be offered to vouchsafe for the nation. And immediately, G-d assented, and gave the Torah to the Jewish people as an eternal inheritance.

Thus, our children became more than children. They became the guarantors of our survival, the links to our future, as our sages taught—the builders of our world.

Given this background, it would have been inconceivable for a Jewish father to be too busy for his children, to shirk his responsibilities, or to relegate them to others. "And ye shall teach it to your children" (*Deuteronomy* 6:7) was not theory, a passage from the Scriptures, but the living imperative that gave meaning to man's every day. It was the father who was entrusted with initiating his child into the world of the Jew. It was he who taught him his first words: "Moses commanded us the Torah. It is an eternal inheritance of the Congregation of Jacob" (*Deuteronomy* 33:4).

More than education, it was a way of life that a father had to impart, and it was precisely because of this that he, and only he, could transmit it. A legacy that is to fortify a child throughout his life, that is to accompany him in old age, that is to be transmitted to future generations, can only be bequeathed in loving kindness by a father. Our rituals, our ceremonies, are there to enhance this special father-child relationship. The Passover Seder, wherein the father is not only called upon to relate the tale, but more important, to encourage the children to ask questions; the Sabbath, when the father reviews with his children the Biblical portion of the week, and where, upon returning from synagogue, he lovingly places his hands upon their heads and blesses them, invoking the ancient blessing of the patriarchs; and Yom Kippur, the most awesome day of all, when every man stands in judgment before G-d, and the father is invited to intercede on behalf of his children by bestowing upon them a special blessing for a year of good life.

In homes where the spirit of these rituals was cherished, the father-child relationship was marked by a special understanding and was free of the tensions which separate the generations. Instead of each going off in his own direction, father and son were united by a common bond—to serve G-d. Thus, what started out as a walk to the synagogue ended as an eternal walk on the road of life, spanning the centuries, joining parent and child into one.

They walked together, the two of them,
Abraham and Isaac as one.

(*Genesis* 22:18)

This devotion to children became so much a part of our people that even the most revered men, occupying the most prestigious positions, were committed to it.

It is told that one Yom Kippur, Rabbi Yisroel Salanter, the renowned nineteenth-century sage, failed to appear at synagogue. The congregation became apprehensive and sent out search parties to find their beloved leader, but there was no trace of him anywhere.

As time passed and the rabbi still did not come, the people decided that they had no option but to start the services. As they concluded and were about to go home, the rabbi finally walked in. There was great rejoicing and much speculation as to where he could have been. All sorts of rumors were circulating. Perhaps, the people whispered, the rabbi, through his mystical powers, had ascended to the very Heavens, or perhaps he had met the prophet Elijah. Anxiously, they waited for their rabbi to speak and reveal the secret.

"On my way to synagogue," the rabbi explained, "I heard a baby cry. The poor child was crying so relentlessly that I became convinced that something was wrong. Sure enough, when I investigated, I found that the little one had been left all alone while his mother went to synagogue. Now, I couldn't leave the baby alone in the house, so I stayed with him until his mother returned."

The people were aghast. Their rabbi had actually been babysitting on Yom Kippur night! "Some Heaven the rabbi ascended to," a congregant sneered sarcastically.

"But he did," replied an old man. "He reached even greater heights. He penetrated the Holy of Holies and secured for us a year of blessing. Almighty G-d," the old man continued, "if our rabbi had compassion on the cry of one little child, comforted him and raised him in his arms, how much more so must You have mercy on us and lift us from our suffering."

Yes, such were the great men of Israel who, despite their revered positions, remained sensitive to the cry of one little child, who perceived that to love G-d is to love His children, that one cannot love one without loving the other.

As a small child, I never considered that there was anything remarkable about the story of Rabbi Yisroel Salanter. My own father would have done the same. No matter how pressured he may have been, he always found time for us, as he did for all other children. My father was never too busy to tell us stories, to say our night prayers, to tuck us into bed with a kiss, a hug, and a "sleep well, my precious ones." And to this very day, whenever I say the *Shema*, I hear my father's voice softly calling, inviting angels to surround my bedside, and G-d Himself to watch over me.

In the name of the G-d of Israel,
On my right side stands the Angel Michael
On my left, Gavriel, before me Uriel, behind me Raphael,
And above me is the spirit of the Almighty Himself.

(Night Prayer)

It was this prayer which lulled me to sleep night after night.

Today I have my own children, and today it is my husband who transmits the language of prayer to my sons and daughters. From the time they were born, it was he who revealed to them the many wonders and mercies of our G-d. By the time they were three years old, they knew every Bible story and were able to recognize the letters of the *aleph beit* and even recite their prayers by heart. Thus, my husband, their father, engraved with love the word of G-d upon their hearts.

The contemporary male would probably have difficulty identifying with such sensitivity to children. Like Harold, he has been conditioned to believe that the exemplary husband and father is the man who can provide the "good life" for his family, and sees no reason to further involve himself. Good-naturedly he announces, "My wife handles all family affairs, I just pay the bills."

This same man, however, who nonchalantly washes his hands of his children, would never apply this logic to the all-important area of his business. Yet he hopes that somehow his children will grow up and thrive without his personal guidance. Such an attitude is not only unrealistic, but betrays the superficiality of the contemporary father-child relationship which is based upon the buying of things rather than upon the giving of self; the showering of luxuries, rather than the acceptance of the responsibility that goes with molding and shaping the hearts of children. Even when such fathers try to communicate on a personal level, they are pathetically inept. Not having been conditioned to relate to their children in spiritual terms, they have precious little to convey, and therefore will take the kids out to be entertained by others. Be it a ballgame, a show, or dinner, the object is to be diverted so that there is no need to confront the sterility of their relationship.

Andy was nine years old when he and my son became close friends. Since their school schedules were different, my Oshie in *yeshiva*, parochial school, and Andy in public school, they didn't have much time to play. Nevertheless, Andy would show up at our house every night like clockwork, and sit by silently while my son did his homework and studied Biblical passages with his father.

My children's friends have always been welcome in our home, but it came to a point where I began to wonder whether Andy's parents might not resent his spending so much time in our house. One day, I met Andy's father in the shopping center. Immediately, I perceived that my intuition had served me right. He made some sarcastic remarks about Andy preferring our house even to going out to dinner Sunday night.

Unfortunately, Andy's father never bothered to ask himself what it was that drew his son to our home, how it was that the boy was happy to sit for hours listening while my husband taught Biblical passages. And so, he continued to relate to his son in the same tired manner as before: a ballgame, dinner out, etc., and refused to accept the fact that it was not a day *out* that Andy lacked, but a day *in* with his father. Having nothing to communicate, they became strangers who lived in one house, but other than that had nothing more in common.

The rapid proliferation of cults, the fascination with gurus, attest to the vacuum left by fathers who have abdicated their authority. Young people are desperately searching for a father figure, and in their yearning embrace anyone who comes along. It will take nothing short of a cultural revolution to make the contemporary male aware of his responsibility toward his children and restore fatherhood to its time-honored place.

Neal was seventeen years old when he first came to my attention. He had been caught taking drugs, and at one point he was even found stealing. His father beat the hell out of him, but nothing seemed to help.

"What can I do with the animal?" he asked me.

"I'll give you the same advice that a sage once gave a father with a similar problem," I said. " 'Go home and love him more.' "

Neal's father became furious. My advice was not to his liking. He refused to understand that you can't beat character and goodness into a child's heart, that these qualities must be imparted through love and kindness.

The sad fact that emerges from both these stories is that, nowadays, very few men know how to be fathers.

"Honor your father and mother" is not only an injunction upon children, but is a warning to all parents to conduct themselves in such a manner that their offspring will find it possible to honor them. Fathers like Neal's who bully rather than love, and fathers like Andy's who entertain rather than guide, can never hope to gain the respect of their children.

It is not for naught that the Bible commands, "Honor your father and mother," rather than love your parents, for where respect abides, love can follow, but the reverse is not always true. Horsing around, allowing children to use a parent's first name, may at first glance seem to build for a warm camaraderie, but ultimately, such freedom is bound to result in disrespect and abuse.

The authentic role model for the Jewish father is Abraham, who bequeathed to us that legacy of loving kindness. Although he was well on in years when his son Isaac was born, it is written that the hearts of father and son were perfectly attuned to one another. Abraham was chosen to be the "Architect of the Jewish People" because he was the perfect parent.

> For I have chosen him, G-d declared, so that he might teach his children and his household after him.
> (*Genesis* 18:19)

Abraham's loving kindness, however, is not to be confused with an abdication of parental authority. He was there to teach, to guide, and to discipline. But there is a special way in which this discipline must be dispensed: "With the left hand (the weaker arm), you push away, but with the right, you immediately draw near" (*Talmud Sanhedrin* 107b).

Punishment, our sages warned, must at all times be tempered with kindness, so that even as the child is being rebuked, he will realize that it is not he, but his conduct, that is being censured. To nag or threaten is not only counterproductive, but fosters neuroses and retards emotional development. The Talmud cites the example of a youngster who, fearing the wrath of his father, actually committed suicide.

Not too long ago, a mother called me in hysterics. Her son had failed to come home from school and was nowhere to be found. We called the police, and fortunately, the child was discovered sleeping in the park. Later we found out that he had received his report card that day and had failed algebra. Remembering his father's threat, "I'll kill you if you flunk math!", he decided to leave home.

Children have a tendency to exaggerate, and not all of them can differentiate between empty threats and reality. Therefore, our sages cautioned us never to threaten punishment, but to dispense immediate discipline, without intimidation or harassment. Abusive language and browbeating have never resolved any problems. If anything, such methods leave children permanently scarred. Moreover, our rabbis warned us never to enforce punishment in moments of anger, for if we are not in control, the child becomes a whipping boy for our frustrations. Discipline, if it is to be effective, must be dispensed within a framework of loving kindness, for that is the only way that its teaching will be lasting.

In all my years, I never heard my father shout, lose his temper, or say an unkind word. If we didn't behave, as was often the case, my father would admonish us by softly saying, "My *teire kinderlach*, my precious children, this type of behavior is not worthy of you."

These words cut us to the quick and made a deeper

impression than any beating or punishment, for they reminded us that we were the trustees of that promise given so many years ago at Sinai. As I grew older, I came to appreciate the simple beauty inherent in this disciplinary measure. Instead of dragging us down and making us feel that we were nothing, my father made us feel that, through our behavior, we actually had the power to bring honor to G-d.

This ideal of *Kiddush Hashem,* honoring G-d's Name, was the basis of all our discipline and is at the core of our religion. As children we knew that we had to do well because we were Jews, because of the pledge given at Sinai, and if we fell short, it was not we who failed, but the Name of G-d was desecrated as well. Admittedly, this is a heavy burden for small children to carry, but challenges can only spur you on to greater heights. They have never broken anyone. It is those who are raised without guidelines, without direction, who end up drifting aimlessly and disintegrating.

We were never troubled by self-doubt. Questions which agonize young people today: "Who am I? What am I? What is it all about?" never bothered us. We always had a sense of ourselves. G-d had entrusted us with His Commandments, and to fulfill them was to sanctify His Name, the highest goal that we could aspire to. My husband and I raised our four children by this dictum, and they have never lost sight of it.

As a case in point, let me share with you a very small but telling incident that occurred when my youngest, Osher Anshil, named after the *Menuchos Osher,* was eight years old. I asked him to run to the supermarket across the street for a bottle of orange juice. He returned emptyhanded, explaining that they were out of the brand that we usually use.

"Well, then, go get another brand," I instructed, and sent him right back. In his haste, he left some money behind, and when he reached the cashier, he was twenty-four cents short.

Terribly embarrassed, he ran home. "I have to go right back," he said, "I owe them twenty-four cents. They might think I forgot the money, and that would be a terrible *chillul Hashem*, desecration of G-d's Name."

What my little boy meant, although he did not articulate it in so many words, was that he didn't want to leave the impression that he, a Jew, who studies and lives by G-d's Bible, would ever be guilty of short-changing someone. A child who has such perception does not have to be shouted at, slapped, or threatened, for his control comes from within. Even when his parents are not around, he will follow the right course, for his discipline has been internalized.

In reaching out to cult children and to youngsters who have gone bad, it is this challenge that I always present. "You come from a nation of prophets," I tell them. "Your people willingly underwent every sacrifice to uphold the Commandments of G-d. Do not betray that trust."

At first, they are taken aback, but then, as the challenge takes hold of them, a transformation also takes place. Suddenly, there is something to aspire to. They are not just crazy lost kids, or bums on the street. They are trustees of Sinai. They have a heritage to follow.

There are, however, exceptional instances, when despite all the good intentions and sacrifices of parents, children remain rebellious. My grandfather, Rabbi Tzvi Hirsh Kohn, may his memory be for a blessing, once told me a story about the Rabbi of Tzernovitz, who had such a rebellious son. The members of the congregation were so outraged by the boy's conduct that they appointed a committee to take the matter up with the rabbi himself. They were certain that once he was made aware of the problem, he would banish his son from the community.

When they came to their rabbi's house, they found him immersed in penitential prayers.

"Almighty G-d," the rabbi's voice came piercing through

the door. "I know full well that we, Your people, are not deserving of Your favor. I admit that we have transgressed Your Commandments, but nevertheless, I beseech You to bless us with a year of goodness and plenty. And should You argue that I have no basis on which to make such a request, then I will tell You frankly that others may not, but I, the Rabbi of Tzernovitz do, for I, too, am a father, and my son has also rebelled against me. And yet, I tell You, my G-d, that if someone were to suggest that I disown him, that I cast him away from my sight, I would throw that man out, for *no matter what, he is my son.*"

The members of the committee, hearing the prayer of their rabbi, trembled with shame. Without even uttering a word, they left.

Now, unbeknown to the rabbi and to the committee, the errant son also heard his father's prayer. Unable to contain himself, he broke down and wept inconsolably. In the midst of his tears, the boy made a silent vow, and swore to justify his father's unbounded love.

The agony and suffering that goes with raising children is not unique to any generation. Long before the Rabbi of Tzernovitz, our patriarch Isaac was similarly afflicted, yet it is written that "Isaac loved Esau" (*Genesis* 25:28). Now surely the Bible does not have to tell us that a father loves his son, and yet we find this emphasis so that parents in every generation may draw strength from it and remember that even when the gift of children is accompanied by pain, even then it is a gift, and we must continue to love them, simply because they are ours.

A man from a well-known family called me. He was beside himself. His sixteen-year-old son had got mixed up with a juvenile gang, was arrested, and was now out on probation.

"Tell me something about your son," I said. "Is he contrite? Does he regret what he did?"

"To be honest, Rebbetzin," he answered, "that is why I'm calling you. I can't get a word out of him, and I hoped that maybe you could talk to him."

"Did you ever see tears in his eyes?" I asked. "Did you ever see him cry?"

For a moment, there was silence at the other end of the wire. "I can't recall," came the hesitant answer, "at least not since he was a very little boy."

"Well," I told the father, "it will be difficult. Eyes that cannot cry usually shield hearts of stone. But nevertheless, I will try."

The boy came to see me, and as I had thought, he was tough. After hours of conversation, we finally started to become friends, and he promised to come to one of my classes. On the day that I was supposed to see him again, he called, and I immediately sensed that something was wrong.

"Rebbetzin," he said, "will you believe me if I tell you something?"

"Of course I will," I assured him.

"I was coming to your class and my friend offered to lend me his car. Maybe I was on the road for five minutes, when the cops pulled me over. I didn't know it, but it was a stolen car. I'm calling you from the police station. Do you still believe me?"

"Yes," I answered, although in my heart I wasn't quite certain. But the story of Tzernovitz had remained with me. As I assured him that I trusted him, for the first time his voice broke and he wept.

"But my father will never believe me," he sobbed, "he will never believe me."

I tried to tell him that he was wrong, that I myself would call his father, but I couldn't convince him.

When I called his father and related the story, he started to rant and rave. "He's just no good. He can just rot in jail! For all I care, they can put him away!"

I told the father the story of the Rabbi of Tzernovitz, but he wasn't impressed. After much argument, he agreed to bail the boy out, but he acted as if he was doing *me* a favor.

"It won't work that way," I told him. "You must show him some sign of love and motivate him to become a true son of his people. Why else should he try? If you treat him like a criminal, he will remain one."

As I worked with the father and his son, the source of their problem became evident. The boy was not too bright and did not do too well in school. The father couldn't accept his son's limitations. He pressured him to the point where the boy gave up and decided to become what the father had always said he was, "a no good bum."

Luckily, the story has a happy ending. Today this young man is gainfully employed, a good husband, and the father of two children. But there are many others who remain permanently crippled by well-intentioned fathers who do not know how to be fathers.

Parental love demands that each child be allowed to grow up to realize his own potential and not be pressed to achieve that which is beyond his capacity. Our father Abraham was sensitive to these innate differences, and imposed upon his children only such responsibility as he felt they could fulfill. Of Isaac he demanded great sacrifice, a life of discipline and dedication to Torah. But of the sons of the concubines he asked only that they avoid what was impure and immoral.

Surely Abraham, whose entire life centered around the Torah, would have desired that all his children be learned of the Law. For him to have made such a request of one child and not of the others would seem to be totally out of character. But Abraham understood that while all the children were his, not all of them were endowed with the same capabilities.

If a man truly loves his son, he will follow the example

set by Abraham. This is a lesson that every father must learn if he is to raise children who will lead meaningful and constructive lives. Not every child can become an Isaac; not every child is capable of spiritual greatness, but *every child* can be taught to live by the laws of morality and cherish compassion and justice.

Instead of pressuring sons to achieve scholastically, fathers would do well to pressure them to become better people. Instead of demanding that they cram information into their heads, they should be taught to develop character and goodness, for in the long run that is the only thing that matters. Whether they mature into honest and dignified individuals will not be contingent on their professions, nor upon their becoming doctors or lawyers, but on whether they have internalized that discipline and wisdom given so many thousands of years ago at Sinai.

🍃

ten

RAISING CHILDREN
WITHOUT JEALOUSY

EVERYONE IN OUR COMMUNITY envied the Goldenbergs. They were a warm, loving family, who always kept together and never seemed to have any problems. Then, one day, Mrs. Goldenberg fell ill, and overnight the family drew apart.

Who should care for her? Who should pay the bills? In whose home should she stay and for how long? Everything became an issue, and by the time old Mrs. Goldenberg passed away, the children barely talked to one another.

During the *shiva*, mourning period, I tried to reconcile them, but they kept bickering. Finally, seeing that I had no recourse, I decided to be blunt: "You keep arguing about who did more for mom, but let's get straight to the point. What made you want to take care of her in the first place?" I asked.

Taken aback by the obviousness of my question, they hesitated for a moment, and then matter of factly answered, "Because she was our mother."

"Well, that's what I thought," I nodded, "but if that's the case, why should it bother you who took care of her and for how long, as long as she was taken care of?"

Embarrassed by my implications of jealousy, they tried to change the subject and spoke of the love they each had for their mother. But once again I interrupted and told them that, with all due respect, it appeared to me that the love of which they spoke was more like "chicken" than "mother love."

Totally baffled by my allusion, they fell silent, and I proceeded to explain.

"What does it mean when someone says, 'I love chicken'?

"Does it mean that this person is willing to devote his life to caring for that chicken, that he's willing to feed it, bathe it, pamper it, and tend to its every need? Or does 'I love chicken' mean that he wishes to eat that chicken, to consume it for his own satisfaction?

"Chicken love, as you can see, is exploitive.

" 'Do for me,' 'Please me.' 'Satisfy me.' "

Such love thrives on demands and is tainted by jealousy. Even as you, those who are consumed by it, are never at peace, because their love is reduced to a ledger sheet of debits and credits.

"But mother love, human love, is different. There, it doesn't matter who does what or when. The pleasure comes from giving, not from taking, from serving, not from consuming and there is never a fear of 'being had.'

"So how do you see it, friends," I asked, "what would you term your relationship? mother love or chicken love?"

It was a bitter pill for the Goldenbergs to swallow, and they would probably have been more resentful of my analogy were it not for the fact that I warned that their attitude was being absorbed by their children, and if not rectified, would one day backfire on them.

Is the story of the Goldenbergs atypical, or is their family strife a natural consequence of sibling rivalry? Moreover, is it possible to overcome jealousy, or are our relationships doomed to end in envy and animosity?

The Bible testifies that the heart of man is evil from youth on (*Genesis* 8:21), which leads us to believe that brotherly love is not easily acquired, but must be cultivated and worked on. Unfortunately, it does not appear that we, or for that matter, our ancestors, have succeeded in any great measure in this regard.

Sibling rivalry prompted Cain to kill his brother, Abel. Sibling rivalry led the brothers to sell Joseph, and it was hatred between brother and brother that led to the destruction of our Holy Temple in Jerusalem. And to this very day, it is hatred that continues to eat away at our innards, consuming our families and our nation as well.

What hope is there? How is it possible to instill that special love in the breast of man so that he may overcome his natural proclivity for jealousy and hatred?

In contrast to chicken love, in our home, love was never a commodity to be bartered. It would never have occurred to my parents to threaten us with, "If you don't behave, mommy and daddy won't love you anymore."

The love of my parents was total and unconditional. They loved us for no better reason than that we were their children, the apple of their eyes, the sum total of their existence, and this told us that their love would remain constant and would never be affected by our behavior.

It would have been inconceivable for us to imagine that our parents would wish to get away from us, even for a weekend, that we were disrupting their relationship, or that we were in any way unwanted. By loving us so completely, by sacrificing for our sake, my parents taught us our first lesson in true love: To find joy in giving rather than exploiting, in sharing rather than indulging, and in placing the needs of others above our own.

It was this attitude which enabled my brothers and me to overcome sibling rivalry and relate to one another without resentment. Although I must admit that even if subconsciously we did harbor such weakness, my parents would never have allowed it to come to the fore.

"How can you be envious of a brother or a sister?" my

178 The Jewish Soul on Fire

mother would have asked incredulously. To her, jealousy was as alien a concept as stealing or lying.

My parents did not believe that it was psychologically unsound to teach children to suppress their emotions. Nor did they subscribe to the advice of professionals who encourage children to talk and act out their hostilities. Their principles were clearly delineated by the Bible: "Thou shalt not covet."

Instinctively, my mother perceived that the child who is allowed to act out his angers (batter dolls or other inanimate objects) will never be taught to control his baser instincts. And worse, as he reaches adulthood, his family and friends might just become his new victims.

I was lecturing on this subject to a group of young mothers, when a woman raised her hand. "My eleven-year-old is jealous of his younger sister," she said. "We are very careful to treat them equally, but no matter what we do, my son keeps complaining. How do you think we should handle it, Rebbetzin?"

"Teach him the Tenth Commandment, 'Thou shalt not covet,'" I said.

"Just like that?" she asked, shocked.

"Yes, just like that," I answered right back.

"Oh, but I couldn't!"

"Why not?" I asked. "Do you teach him not to lie, not to cheat, not to hurt? Then why can't you teach him not to be jealous?"

"I don't want him to develop a complex. I don't want him to feel guilty," she said.

"The guilt that you are so afraid of is probably the best thing you could instill in your son. It will teach him to control his jealousies and develop his conscience. Believe me," I went on, "there is no amount of attention that can calm a jealous child, for it is not what he *lacks*, but what *others have*, that he desires. And so, the more you indulge him, the more convinced he will be that his accusations are justified."

"Thou shalt not covet" is the last of the Ten Commandments. The word of G-d is clear and precise. There are no ifs, buts, or extenuating circumstances. G-d actually demands that we extricate all traces of envy from our hearts (even if such denial leaves us with unresolved conflicts). The Commandment of G-d stands above and beyond all rationalizations. It transcends the centuries. It is independent of cultural bias, and it does not require professional approbation. It calls out to man, charging him to summon his inner strength and better himself.

"Thou shalt not covet," our sages teach, encompasses all the Commandments, for it is when a man covets that which he does not possess that he becomes capable of hatred, theft, and even murder. It is covetousness that is at the root of all evil, and it is covetousness that perverts love into greed, reducing it to an exploitive experience. And yet, this is the one Commandment that we are afraid to impress on our children. Not only do we refrain from teaching, "Thou shalt not covet," but we have actually legitimized it. "It's natural to be jealous," we say, and with that glib statement we dismiss the Commandment. Nevertheless, the conflicts and the tensions remain, and as we try to resolve them, we encounter further frustration and failure, for the equality formula never works.

Despite the assurances of our Declaration of Independence, all men are *not* created equal, and for parents to pretend otherwise is dishonest. We are not the same in intellect, appearance, or talent. Moreover, there are children who are engaging, and others who get under your skin. A child may have a winning smile and resemble a beloved relative, or he may have the disposition and appearance of someone the parent dislikes. In any event, to foster the fiction that everyone is equal is hypocritical, and children are the first to see through it.

A boy of seventeen who was flunking out of high school

came to see me with his parents. At first, it was difficult to pinpoint his problem. To all appearances, his parents were sensitive, educated people, committed to his welfare.

"My Keith is a very fine boy," the mother volunteered. "His only problem is that he doesn't try hard enough."

Keith had an older brother in law school, and his parents assumed that he would go the same route, but Keith couldn't make it.

"If only he would apply himself," his mother kept insisting, "I know that he would succeed."

It took a long time for her to comprehend that it was not Keith who had to apply himself, but *she* who needed reorientation. She had to learn that each child was different, that although she had provided equal opportunities for both her sons, they could not avail themselves of those opportunities in exactly the same manner, that more went into making a lawyer than a trust fund for his education.

Deep down in his heart, Keith was only too painfully aware of his limitations. He realized that no matter how hard he worked, he would never get there. His mother's good intentions backfired. The more she insisted that he try, the sharper the contrast between the boys became, until Keith ended up hating his brother.

Keith not only failed to appreciate his mother's attempts at impartiality, but he accused her of favoritism and bias. His mother, of course, denied these allegations, but secretly worried that there might be some truth to them, for while she loved both her sons equally (if love of children is to be understood as the wish to see them happy and well), she could not take equal pride in their achievements. It is this lack of pride which Keith sensed and interpreted as rejection.

It emerges that despite the sincerest of efforts, the child who is convinced that he is not being treated fairly will always find something to complain about. There is no amount of attention that will reassure him, or of gifts that will satisfy him. He is a descendent of Cain, who had the whole world before him and yet could not bear to see his brother's success.

Such examples abound, not only among children, but in adult life as well. I remember a woman becoming frantic when her sister decorated her home and installed a kitchen similar to hers. Now, this woman already had her own beautiful kitchen, so why should she have begrudged her sister? When I tried to question her, she skirted the issue and attempted to camouflage her resentment with some meaningless, psychology-laced jargon.

"It's not that I begrudge her," she insisted, "but I want to be my own person without my sister copying my every act."

To a certain extent, such feelings are familiar to all of us. We can deal with anonymous strangers wearing identical pieces of jewelry or driving the same model car, but we become irritated if an acquaintance does the same. We will, of course, never admit to envy. We are quick to rationalize our resentment by protesting that it is our individuality that we wish to protect. Basically, however, it is jealousy that blinds our vision and leaves us tormented and discontented.

It appears that neither equality nor equal opportunity have proven effective antidotes to envy and greed. What's more, the story of Joseph demonstrates that our forefathers did not fare too well, either. Nevertheless, we must seek our answer in the Bible, for it is only there that we can discover perfect truth, formulas for life which have passed the test of time and which come from G-d Himself.

Study of the Bible will demonstrate a disregard for our contemporary outlook on equality and fairness. It is not only the patriarch Jacob who appears to show favoritism to Joseph by bestowing upon him a coat of many colors, but

G-d Himself seems to prefer Abel's offering over Cain's. And even more puzzling is Moses' apportioning of the Holy Land. The territories that he assigns to the tribes not only vary in size and natural resources, but the tribe of Levi is denied land altogether.

Moreover, G-d divided our entire nation into three separate and distinct groups: Kohen, Levi, and Yisrael, with prerogatives, obligations, and responsibilities that are different and not interchangeable. The Torah does not apologize for these inequities. Males, females, first borns, minors, are all assigned unequal but *unique* roles, which emphasize individuality rather than uniformity. Obviously, G-d wished to teach us that contentment is not to be found in aspiring to sameness, but in discovering our own uniqueness.

By emphasizing uniqueness over equality, Jewish Law diminishes rivalry and encourages each person to develop according to his own potential. However where equality is stressed, competition is also intensified, with each individual attempting to prove himself by outdoing the other. It is in this mad rush to establish superiority that jealousy and greed are generated.

The Torah never idealized the competitive spirit. We are called upon to be only ourselves and no one else. Rabbi Zushya expressed this ideal when he stated:

"I shall not fear if the Almighty G-d asks me why I did not acquire the Torah learning of Moses. I shall simply answer, 'Heavenly Father, You did not endow me with the brilliant mind of our teacher.' "Nor shall I be concerned," he continued, "if He asks me why I did not demonstrate the compassion of Abraham. I shall frankly tell Him that He did not grant me the nobility of soul with which He blessed the patriarch. And if He should ask me why I did not compose psalms in praise of His Holy Name as David did, even then I shall not fear. I will reply that I was not given the gifts of David. But if He should ask me, 'Zushya, why were you not like Zushya could have been?', then I shall tremble, for I will have no answer."

That is all that is required of a man—to realize his own potential, to live his life to the fullest, and to use the unique talent with which G-d endowed him for the benefit of mankind.

Whether we can be free of the ugly pangs of jealousy will in great measure depend upon whether our parents will have the wisdom and the love to raise us with this perception and allow us to be ourselves and no one else.

But if our solution is not in equality or sameness, how then can we resolve the murderous act of Cain and the selling of Joseph?

Contrary to popular belief, it was not G-d's preferring Cain to Abel that led Cain to kill his brother. The disease of jealousy had been festering in Cain's heart from childhood on. Like his mother, he could not bear to see anything exist that he could not possess, and like his father, who tried to shift blame for his weakness ("The woman whom You gave unto me, she gave me of the tree, and I did eat." *Genesis* 3:12), Cain, too, refused to accept responsibility for his heinous act and declared, "Am I my brother's keeper?" (*Genesis* 4:9). Cain absorbed his parents' attitude and compounded it with his own selfish hatred.

The story of Joseph is also fraught with family conflict. Joseph was the son of Jacob's beloved Rachel, while his brothers (except for Benjamin) were the sons of Leah, who had been forced upon Jacob in marriage. As the children of the less-loved wife, the brothers always felt inferior and inadequate. Even before Joseph was born, they hated him for no other reason than that he was the son of Rachel.

When children witness tension between their parents, they get caught up in the hostility and feel justified in exacting vengeance for the parent whom they feel was wronged. It is this hatred which prompted the brothers to heartlessly soak Joseph's coat in a pool of blood and present it to their elderly father. The hurt that the brothers felt for their mother, Leah, was of such intensity that it obscured their love and led them to the perfidious act of selling their brother.

Joseph was perhaps the loneliest of children. Orphaned, shunned by his brothers, he yearned for acceptance, and in desperation even resorted to childish boasting. But his boasting as well as his coat of many colors was the *result*, and not the cause, of a house already divided.

To be sure, the polygamy that divided Jacob's household no longer exists, but conflicts continue to separate husbands and wives, and it is these frictions that contribute to sibling rivalry. More than inequality, it is parental discord that feeds the flames of jealousy. Children who are raised in homes where love becomes a commodity to be bartered, where parents are divided, will absorb these tensions. Given these conditions, the most innocuous item can become a "coat of many colors," bringing forth all the jealousies which plagued Jacob's household. Where, however, parents are united in their devotion to their children, their love inspires confidence and assures each child that he has his own unique place within the family unit.

It was this love which my own parents communicated to us and which kept us together even under the most trying circumstances.

Soon after the occupation, the Nazis announced that we would have to be relocated. Adults, they said, would have to march on foot, but children would be given transport. In those days, we were not yet fully aware of the extent of German treachery, and we actually believed their lie.

As my mother readied us for the trip, one of our neighbors came to beg a favor. She asked to borrow my little brother's stroller for her crippled daughter.

Without hesitation, my mother gave it to her, assuring

herself that we wouldn't need it since we would be traveling by truck.

But the trucks never came.

It was bitter cold, and we were alone, hungry, and inadequately dressed. My four-year-old little brother was feverish, and my older brother, Yankie, who was only ten at the time, had to carry him for miles on his shoulder, while dragging me along as well.

In retrospect, I have often wondered how he did it, how he, who was a mere child, became a parent overnight. From whence did he summon the strength to forget his own pain and take care of us, his little brother and sister?

The answer is the love of my parents.

It is written in our ancient books that, at the beginning of time, the Almighty went forth in search of a place where He might build His Sanctuary.

Where should it be? Which city should He choose?

In the Holy City of Jerusalem there lived two brothers. Their houses were at opposite ends of the city, and they were separated by a great mountain. Now, one brother was very poor, but blessed with children, while the other possessed a great fortune, but had no family.

One night, the wealthy brother tossed and turned in his sleep.

It is terribly unjust, he thought to himself, that I should be given so much, while my brother has so little.

That same night, the poor brother also awoke from his sleep. Of what good is all my brother's money? he thought to himself, Without children his life must be lonely and meaningless.

And as the brothers lay awake thinking of how they might give comfort to one another, they both came up with an identical plan. In the darkness of the night, each would secretly leave a gift at the door of his brother.

And so, the two brothers set out and began to climb the

mountain from opposite directions. And as they reached the top, they suddenly lighted upon one another. For a moment, they just stood there, overwhelmed by shock, and then, weeping with joy, they fell into each other's arms. And as they embraced, a Heavenly Voice was heard:

"This ground has been sanctified by the love of the brothers. It is here that I shall build My Holy Temple."

For centuries, the Temple stood in Jerusalem in majestic splendor, enveloping in love all those who would come to pray there. And then, one day, the love of the brothers turned into hatred, and the Holy Sanctuary of G-d could no longer stand.

When shall the Temple be rebuilt?

When the brothers shall once again be united by love.

eleven

RELIGIOUS DILEMMAS

WHY DO WE NEED RELIGION?

Why did G-d have to burden us with so many Commandments?

Isn't it possible to be moral, ethical, and compassionate without religious tenets?

Phil Wagner was the proprietor of a local hardware store. He prided himself on being a philosopher of sorts, and whenever I shopped in his place, he tried to draw me into a discussion.

"Rebbetzin," he'd start good-naturedly, "give me one good reason why I should be religious, and I'll become a rabbi right away!"

Over the years, I gave up answering Phil, for no matter what I would say, he'd always come back with the same stock argument: "As long as you're a good person, moral, and ethical, that's all the religion that is needed."

Yet it was obvious that Phil didn't feel as confident as he made out to be, for why else would he keep hammering away at religion? And so, from time to time I did make an attempt to reach him, by reminding him of his responsibility to his children.

"Even if not for your sake, you should really come to synagogue for the kids. They need roots, guidelines, something to believe in."

"Oh, don't worry about them," Phil would immediately respond, "they have all the guidelines they need. My kids are straight. They don't need any religion."

Then, one day, I had a phone call. It was Phil. He had to see me right away.

"Don't tell me that you're looking for another debate," I said half-kiddingly.

But there was no laughter in Phil's voice. "Rebbetzin, it's serious. Can I come over?"

Instead of my jovial, teasing friend, the Phil who walked in looked worried and tense.

"What happened?" I asked.

"It's my daughter, Rebbetzin, my beautiful Joanie. I don't know what got into her. You know she was always a good girl, never messed around or anything." Phil was beside himself now. He could hardly control his rage.

"Would you believe it? She moved in with her boyfriend. No marriage, no nothing! They're living together like bums."

"I hate to rub salt in an open wound Phil," I said gently, "but that's exactly what I meant when I spoke about religious guidelines. By today's standards, there's absolutely nothing wrong in living with someone. As far as Joanie is concerned, it's not immoral, and from her point of view, she's right."

Phil became annoyed. He felt that by referring to our old religious debates I was being unfair. But finally, he understood that if Joanie's morality had been based on G-d's Commandments rather than on his views, he would have offered a set of principles which would have helped him persuade her that marriage was the proper course. There would have been no way that she could have justified her actions, for deep down she would have always known that to live with someone without benefit of marriage was wrong, for no other reason than that G-d said so, and that awareness was the leverage that Phil would have needed.

Phil's story is not isolated. Over the years, I have met many individuals like him, people who are convinced that belief in G-d is not necessary to maintain one's values.

But if a man does not recognize a higher authority, if he is the sole arbiter of what is right and wrong, then eventually, he is going to rationalize and compromise. Ideals, morals, principles, and ethics change from society to society, from generation to generation, from culture to culture, and man bends to them even as he bends to the wind. But those whose values are anchored to Divine principles remain unchanging, for they have something to sustain them even when their own will crumbles.

This is not to say that one cannot be highly principled and yet be a non-believer, or that all observant people are moral and ethical. The religious as well as the irreligious are prone to the same weaknesses, but with one fine difference —the believer, even as he falls, is aware that he is falling. He cannot rationalize away G-d's Law, for that which He proclaimed immoral can never become moral, even if the entire world endorses it as such. G-d's Law stands above cultural bias, and the religious man knows it. It is this knowledge that makes the difference, for even as he succumbs, his conscience calls out and demands that he redress the wrong and make amends.

Every man has an Achilles heel, a weak spot which tempts him to rationalize. At such times, it is only the perception that G-d is there that can keep him on the straight and narrow. This holds true not only in regard to morals and ethics, but in other areas as well. For example, the man whose charity and kindness is based on his own whim and desire cannot at all times be counted on. But he whose generosity is founded on G-ds' Law will always respond, for it is not *his own* inclination that motivates him, but the *higher command of G-d.* Therefore, even if he is not in the mood to be generous, he must extend himself, even if he is not inclined toward giving, he must give, and even if he does not want to be compassionate, he must be kind. The truly religious man is good for no other reason than that G-d commands him to be so, and therefore his goodness is constant and lasting.

The story of the illustrious Rabbi of Radin is perhaps the best illustration of the influence which genuine religion can have in shaping and molding a man's character.

It is told that the rabbi would travel from community to community in Poland in order to teach and make his books available to his people. On one occasion, he hired a coachman to take him on a trip. A few miles out of town, the carriage suddenly came to a halt.

"Rabbi," the wagon driver called, "do me a favor. I want to get some hay for my horse. Keep a sharp lookout and make sure nobody sees me. If anyone comes, just yell!"

With that, the coachman ran to the field, but no sooner had he gathered a large bundle of hay than the rabbi shouted: "Someone sees! Someone sees!"

In a panic, the coachman dropped his bundle, ran to the carriage, and drove off at a gallop. After a few minutes, he looked back to see who was watching. Realizing that no one was in sight, he became incensed, and turning to the rabbi demanded: "What are you trying to do, make a fool of me? There is nobody here and you know it. No one saw me."

"You're mistaken," the rabbi replied calmly. There *is* SOMEONE here, SOMEONE who sees." And he pointed his finger Heavenward.

And that is the essence of true religion—to be so keenly aware of G-d that you become conscious of His presence everywhere, in the privacy of your home, in your place of business, and in your social encounters. Once you develop such a faith, it is not likely that you will compromise or that you will succumb to the pressures of your environment, for you are always aware of that everseeing eye of G-d.

But the end-goal of religion cannot be mere mastery of ethics and morality. There must be something more to life, something that goes beyond being nice and decent, something that allows us to rise above our mundane existence. If religion is genuine, if indeed it comes from G-d, it must lead to those spiritual heights.

"And you shall be holy unto Me," is the injunction of the Almighty (*Leviticus* 19:2).

But how can we mere humans actually achieve holiness?

G-d Himself prescribed the formula: "You shall remember and do all My Commandments and be holy unto your G-d" (*Numbers* 15:40).

Herein is to be found the great mystery of religion. The Commandments of G-d generate holiness, and through them, even our most mundane act can become spiritual. The generating force of the *Mitzvot*, Commandments, is so powerful that it links us to G-d throughout our daily lives. Take a simple activity like eating, something that all of us do several times a day without even thinking. Through the Commandments, this ordinary act is elevated to a Divine service and becomes more than mere gratification of appetite. (First we must determine whether the food we eat is kosher, and even then there are rituals which we must perform which prevent us from immediately satiating our hunger. Hands have to be washed, blessings must be recited, meat and milk must be separated, etc.)

These strictures dominate every aspect of our Jewish life and invest even our most automatic acts with a higher purpose so that we may find a meaning that goes beyond mere toiling, eating, drinking, and reproducing.

There are those, however, who would cynically question whether anything could exist outside of these earthly pleasures.

"As far as I'm concerned, I live for today," an acquaintance once told me. "I tried going to synagogue a few times," he admitted, "but I didn't get any highs. I didn't even enjoy it, so I may as well take in what I can, when I can."

"You remind me of the beggar in the House of Rothschild," I told him. And with that, I proceeded to tell him the story.

"The House of Rothschild was renowned for its hospitality. No one was ever sent away emptyhanded, and so, one day, when a beggar came knocking at the door of the Rothschilds, he was immediately invited in, seated at the table, and offered a meal. The poor man sat there all agog, unable to believe his eyes. To sit at the table of a Rothschild was more than he ever could have dreamt of.

"And then, something strange occurred. The beggar saw the baroness pick up a bell and ring. Suddenly, the great dining room doors opened, and men dressed in magnificent livery, carrying the most succulent delicacies, entered. Again and again, the baroness picked up the magical bell, and wonder of wonders, the men would reappear.

" 'Ah,' the beggar thought to himself, 'if only I possessed such a bell, how different my life could be!'

"At the close of the meal, Baron Rothschild prepared to give him a gold piece, but the poor fellow decided to play it smart.

" 'Why,' he reasoned, 'should I settle for the usual gold piece? I'll ask for something that will once and for all resolve my problems.'

"Mustering his courage, he blurted out: 'Your honor, I appreciate your kindness, but instead of the gold coin, may I have that wondrous bell from the table?'

"Rothschild smiled quizzically at this strange request, but if that was what the man wanted, that's what he would get.

"Elated, the beggar ran all the way home. 'Wife, wife!' he shouted. 'From now on, we won't have any problems. Wait until you see what I've got. Watch this!' he exclaimed, as he proceeded to ring the bell. But nothing happened. Men in livery did not appear, trays laden with delicacies were nowhere in sight. There was only silence.

"The poor man had no way of comprehending that it was not the *bell*, but the *house* that was different. When the Baroness Rothschild picked up the bell, an army of servants stood by, ready to meet her every wish. But when he rang, the only response was the rattling of empty dishes.

"You are just like that beggar," I told my friend. "Even as he kept ringing the bell hoping for some magic, so you decided to go one day to synagogue and give religion a chance. You sat there, your heart an empty cupboard, ringing furiously, 'Bring me faith!' 'Inspire me!' 'Give me a spiritual high!' Well, it doesn't work that way. Instant religion does not exist."

If religion is no longer a potent force in our lives, if it has lost its effectiveness and can not promote the peace of mind that it offered our ancestors, it is largely due to this confusion between religion and instant gratification. The inner strength accrued from a life lived with faith cannot be acquired overnight. One must sacrifice for it, and more important, be worthy of it. People who go to synagogue hoping for a high will never find it, for it is not G-d they seek, but personal pleasure, and self-indulgence can neither inspire nor ennoble. If anything, it leads to *ennui*, decadence, and ultimately, self-destruction. Hence, the frustration and sense of despair prevalent among so many.

I realize that these are not easy concepts to accept. We are a spoiled generation and have become accustomed to easy living, minimum effort, and quick reward. Rituals which demand self-renunciation are simply not to our liking, and yet, spiritual strength can only be found through discipline, through the actual breaking of our will, even to the point of self-denial. Our rituals, our ceremonies, all lead us in that direction. From infancy, we train our children in them so that they may be masters over their desires rather than be mastered by them. To the uninitiated, it may appear that such structured existence encased in myriad commandments is stifling and burdensome, but in essence, the opposite is true. By disciplining us so totally, G-d endowed us with the ultimate freedom through which we can transcend our own limitations and our own bodily needs.

Freedom is not to be found in abandon, but in control. A man who is bound by his passion, be it sex, drugs, alcohol, gambling, or an obsession with money, is a slave, the victim of his own habits, whose subjugation comes from within the soul. Therefore, his hope for freedom is not to be found in the physical or the material world, but in the liberation of his inner self. It is the anxieties of his mind and the passions of his heart that enslave him, and it is from that bondage that the Laws of G-d come to free him.

"Who is mighty?" our sages ask.

"He who is able to conquer his will, overcome his passions, and subdue his evil inclinations" (*Ethics of the Fathers*, Chapter 4:1).

If a man is endowed with spiritual strength, it will not matter where life takes him. Whether he is incarcerated in a dungeon or pampered in a palace, his spirits will soar upward and he will be free.

Not too long ago, I interviewed such a man on my weekly television program. His name is Iosif Mendelevich. He is a Russian "prisoner of conscience." In introducing him, I referred to him as a "man of might" such as our sages described. But he took exception to my comparison, stating that if he possessed these qualities, all Jews possessed them as well, and I guess, in a sense, he was correct, for the strength of our nation cannot be defined in physical terms. It is not bound by time or place, but is rooted in that ultimate freedom which comes from Sinai and grants man total control.

Nevertheless, the story of Iosif Mendelevich shines forth like a beacon in a world of darkness. Here is a man, born into a communist-atheist society, where to live as a Jew is deemed a crime, where to pursue Jewish studies is an impossible dream, and where the observance of the Commandments entails hazardous risks—and yet, in order to bring the plight of his suffering people to the world, he willingly endangers his life by hijacking a plane (knowing full well that it doesn't stand a chance of reaching Israel).

Sentenced to twelve years at hard labor in the prisons of Russia, he never forgets his Jewishness, works overtime so that he need not desecrate the Sabbath, starves himself rather than eat non-kosher food, and imperils his life in order to pray.

Mendelevich was brutally penalized for clinging so tenaciously to the faith of his fathers, and was sentenced to three additional years of torture. But there was no penalty that they could ever impose upon him that could deprive him of his freedom, for his soul was anchored to Sinai, and no man could imprison it.

Undaunted, he persisted in his Herculean determination to be a Jew. He fashioned a *tallis*, prayer shawl, from an old and tattered scarf, knitted a *yarmulke* from his only pair of gloves, pasted together a prayer book from fragments of letters which he received from his father, and taught himself Hebrew and Torah.

I asked Mendelevich from whence he drew the inner strength that enabled him to rise to such splendid heights.

"From the Covenant between ourselves and G-d," came his ready reply.

"Mr. Mendelevich," I persisted, "during all those years of imprisonment, you must have been dreaming of the day when you would be freed, the things you would do, the places you would visit. What has been your most inspiring moment since leaving Russia?"

"There were many," Mendelevich said smiling, "but perhaps the moment that moved me most was when I came to Hebron, the resting place of the patriarchs."

Degraded, tortured, oppressed, starved, humiliated, cut off from all contact with his family, confined to long years of isolation and loneliness, Mendelevich, when he finally realizes the day of his liberation, does not seek his happiness in indulgence or in fun, but in a dusty village, at the graveside of his fathers, and there he pronounces a prayer which links him to his roots, enabling him to soar upwards to celestial heights, even to Sinai.

Is this indomitable faith the heritage of the few, or can we all take possession of it? Indeed, how does a man find G-d?

A sage once challenged his disciples with this very question.

"Tell me," he asked, "where is G-d?"

His students, taken aback for a moment by the simplicity of the question, responded, "G-d is everywhere."

"No, my children," the sage replied. "G-d is not everywhere. G-d is only where man allows Him to enter."

Those who wish to find faith can do no less then open their hearts to G-d and invite Him to guide them on the road of life.

If G-d is to fortify us with strength, endow us with serenity, and liberate us from our anxieties, we cannot consign Him to a visit to the synagogue, a holiday celebration, or a theological dissertation. Rather, we must make Him the reality of our very existence.

In proclaiming the Ten Commandments, the Almighty calls out, "I am the L-rd your G-d, who brought you forth

from the land of Egypt, from the house of bondage . . ."
(*Exodus* 20:1).

Why, our sages ask, did not G-d introduce Himself as the
Mighty Power who created the heavens and the earth?

And they answer, "To teach you that the Almighty, who
in His infinite love brought you forth from bondage, is your
personal G-d who cares for you and watches over you, and if
you will it, will continue to redeem you, even today."

This is the G-d to whom we call out, "*Hineni*—Here I
am"— and who in turn answers us with "*Hineni*, I have heard
your cry. You are not alone. I am your G-d."

This is the G-d of our fathers, who wipes away our tears,
who heals our wounds, who consoles us in time of bereave-
ment, and imbues us with faith so that we may deal with the
good as well as the bad.

It was this faith that allowed my friend Lilly to confront
life's trials when her husband, Artie (who had been the
president of our synagogue), was suddenly taken from her in
the prime of his life.

Not long after Artie passed away, Lilly came to see me,
terribly agitated.

"I don't know how I did it," she said, plunging into a
chair. "G-d must have put the words into my mouth. I feel as
if I've been through a wringer.

"I was on my way to work," Lilly started to tell me, "and
I was sharing a cab to the railroad station with Bernie
Hendel. You remember him." She paused, looking at me
knowingly.

Oh, yes, I remembered Bernie. How could I forget? He
caused us enough trouble—coming to the synagogue and
riling everybody up against Orthodoxy.

"Well," Lilly continued, "as the cab approached the
Temple, Bernie started his usual *shtick*.

"'That place didn't seem to do Artie any good,' he said,

pointing to the Temple. 'He should have been smart like me. I don't get involved. I don't expect anything, so I don't get hurt. But look at Artie, working his a-- off, and where did it get him? If you ask me, he got a bum deal.'

"His words really cut me," Lilly confided, "I had to fight to keep back the tears, but I couldn't let him get away with it. I made the cabbie stop right in front of the synagogue and decided once and for all to have it out with him.

"You say Artie got a bum deal," I told him. "Well, I don't know about that. True, he died without warning, but then again, he had no pain, he never suffered. He lived his life well and made his exit like a gentleman, and I'm grateful for that.

"The day will come when you, too, will have to go, Bernie. But whether you will be able to go with the dignity, the good name with which Artie went, remains to be seen. So all things considered, I don't think Artie did so badly."

As Lilly finished her story, she anxiously turned to me.

"Rebbetzin, I don't know too much about religion, but I do believe in G-d, and I hope I answered him well."

Lilly not only answered well, but she touched upon basic truths. Death, even as birth, is part of the reality of existence. There is no way that we can avoid it. Therefore, the most that we can hope for is that when G-d calls us, we go without shame or regret.

True, Artie worked for our synagogue, but he had no illusions about bargaining with G-d. He never expected Him to change the laws of nature for his sake. Artie did what he did because he was a good man, and precisely because of that, he was able to make his exit with honor and love.

Lilly and I had many discussions. She told me that while she will never understand why G-d took her Artie away at such a young age, she also had to admit that no matter when He would have called him, it would have been too soon. She reminded me that when her mother had passed away, some unthinking person tried to console her by pointing to her mother's ripe old age.

"I became furious," Lilly said. "To me, it made no difference whether she was sixty or ninety. She was *my* mother, and when she went, it was too soon."

It is always too soon to say good-bye to someone you love, but every relationship does have to come to an end, and only G-d can determine when that time should be and who should be the one to go first. And in a sense, it is better that way, for that is one decision that no human being should have to make.

Lilly told me that very often she would lie awake at night thinking, and it occurred to her that G-d may have chosen Artie to go first to spare him the terrible agony of loneliness.

"Maybe G-d considered me the stronger of the two," she whispered, her eyes brimming with tears.

"To tell you the truth, Rebbetzin, at times I get very angry with G-d for having taken Artie, but in all fairness, I must also recognize that He gave me a great guy while many of my friends ended up with terrible marriages. I guess in the long run it all evens out, and it would be hypocritical to blame Him for one without giving Him credit for the other."

Faith enabled Lilly to understand that it is G-d who authored the script of her life, that although at times she was confused and troubled by it all, He would always be there to pull her through.

This type of faith is not to be confused with passive resignation. Rather, it is an inner strength that enables us to accept life's trials without falling apart. There is no way that any of us can escape the reality of suffering. At one time or another, we are all hit, the rich and the poor, the mighty and the weak. All of us must confront pain, illness, and death, but whether we are able to overcome or not will depend on the quality of our faith.

It is not only through tragedy that our strength of character is tested. The limitations of our inborn traits can be equally challenging. Whether we be short or tall, wise or foolish, attractive or homely, is preordained, and depending on how we fare, we may feel that we have been short-changed, and become resentful and antagonistic. I met a man like that once. He had a mean disposition—he was angry at G-d for not having made him tall, dark, and hand-some. I told him about a Talmudic sage who was so homely that people actually stopped to comment about his ugliness. But the rabbi was never bothered by their remarks. Good-naturedly, he would tell them, "If you have any complaints about my appearance, tell it to the One who created me."

The man I described and the rabbi were equally disad-vantaged, but one became emotionally crippled, while the other managed to overcome his handicap. The rabbi's faith told him that, surely, the Almighty must have had a reason for creating him as He did. Therefore, instead of worrying about the things that were beyond his control, he concen-trated his efforts in areas that were within his sphere of influence.

Talent, ability, intelligence, appearance, all come from G-d, and no man deserves credit for possessing any of these attributes. But how he decides to apply them will depend solely on him, and it is in that area that he will be judged.

For example, a man may be blessed with a brilliant mind, but whether he uses his intellect to eradicate disease or develop germ warfare will be his choice to make. Or a man may be born with leadership qualities, but whether he opts to liberate (as Abraham Lincoln did) or oppress (as Hitler did) will depend entirely on him. Or a man may be endowed with creative ability, but whether he utilizes his creativity to ennoble through art or debase through pornography will once again be a matter of personal choice commensurate with his faith. It is of small significance whether a man decides to become a physician or a cab driver. More important is what sort of doctor or what sort of cab driver he decides to be. It is not the talent or the gifts we possess that count, but how we use those gifts. It is not the fate that befalls us, but how we react to that fate that is crucial. That is why some people are able to cope while others cannot.

This power of faith is so remarkable that it can even convert negative traits into positive ones. The individual who may be inclined toward cruelty may learn to channel his callousness into something worthwhile and choose a profession in which detachment becomes an asset, such as surgery or law enforcement. To be sure, the predisposition is inborn and beyond our control, but whether we aim for goodness or evil, service or self-indulgence, will be influenced by the quality of our faith.

The sages of the Talmud explain that everything is predestined and beyond our control except our *fear* and *reverence of G-d—our faith,* which in Hebrew is called *yirat shamayim* (*Berakhoth* 33:13).

This human capacity for self-determination is always present. Even under the most oppressive circumstances, the choice is always there.

Not too long ago, I was lecturing in Toronto. I was about to begin my speech, when a man came rushing up to me.

"May I have a few minutes of your time?" he asked, in a voice that betrayed a Hungarian accent.

He must have been in his early fifties, which led me to surmise that he was a survivor of Hitler's Holocaust.

"Are you by any chance related to the Rabbi Jungreis who was the Sage of Nadudvar?" he asked.

My heart started to pound, and a thousand memories crowded into my mind.

"The Sage of Nadudvar," I answered slowly, "was my grandfather."

The man's eyes filled with tears, and a smile of relief broke out on his face. "At last I found you! You see, I am from Nadudvar, and your *zeide* was my revered rabbi and teacher. I was at his side when they took him away, but even then, in that terrible moment, he thought only of others. I ran up to him and offered to share some of our bread, but he refused to take it. Instead, he gave me his blessing. I never forgot, and I always hoped that I might transmit his blessing to someone from his family."

Pictures, images, voices, memories, converged on me from the past. I was a little girl again in Nadudvar. I was sitting on my *zeide*'s knees while he swayed back and forth chanting the sweet melody with which he studied the Holy Books. To have known my *zeide* was to have encountered the beauty of holiness in a man. His voice, his manner, his entire being, communicated love and compassion, and although I was a small child when I last saw him, his saintly face, the sound of his voice, have never left me. When the Germans took my *zeide* away, he was carrying my little baby cousin in his arms, and that was the last we heard of him. And now, thirty-six years later, in Toronto, Canada, a man was standing before me, telling me that he brought me blessings from the flames.

Very often, I have thought about that meeting in Toronto and the immortality with which faith can endow a man. My grandfather had no control over the sheer horror and madness that swept over Europe, but even in that hell, he had the freedom of choice to live by his faith or give in to despair. It was because he had the fortitude and the vision to make this choice that thirty-six years later, I, his only surviving granddaughter, living in a new world, on another continent, received his legacy.

The Nazis perished, but my grandfather's faith survived the flames.

This is the tradition that has been bequeathed to me—to kindle the light of faith in every situation, under all circumstances, for in the final analysis, that is the only area in which we humans have control over that which befalls us. Illness, suffering, and death, are, alas, all part of our experience. But whether we allow these tragedies to cripple us, or whether we learn to conquer them, will depend entirely on the quality of our faith, our *Yirat Shamayim*.

Truth be told, everything is preordained. Even before we are born, G-d knows the script of our lives, and in a sense, we are all victims. There is only one real freedom that we have, and that is the attitude with which we choose to live our lives—whether we opt for the light of faith or the darkness of despair will ultimately depend on us.

But how do we find this faith? How do we overcome the great gap between light and darkness?

"How great is that distance?" a man once asked of a sage.

"The distance is as great as that between east and west," the sage replied.

"So far!" the man moaned.

"No, so near," was the answer. "It is just one turn toward light that leads to G-d."

 ‮‮

twelve

FAITH IN THE FLAMES

IT WAS THIS FAITH that enabled me as a small child to survive the horrors of Hitler's Holocaust. I recall standing for hours in the mud of Bergen-Belsen waiting for roll call. When the Nazis finally arrived in their immaculate uniforms and shiny boots, cracking their whips and snapping orders, they appeared almost godlike. Yet strangely enough, I, a little girl dressed in rags, with shaven head and covered with sores, would not have traded places with them for anything. I had only to contrast my father's saintly face with the naked brutality in their eyes to know that it was preferable to die a thousand deaths than to be the daughter of these savages. Although I could not fathom the meaning of the sheer terror that surrounded me, I knew beyond all doubt that G-d could not be a part of it, and that ultimately, we who believed in Him would overcome.

Strangely enough, during that torturous period I never thought of asking where G-d was, nor did I ever hear anyone else voice that question. In this regard, I was perhaps more fortunate than most, for as the daughter of a rabbi, I was surrounded by people who towered larger than life in their zeal to remain loyal to G-d. Day and night, they came to seek my father's guidance.

"How," they asked, "can we circumvent violating the

Sabbath? How can we uphold the laws of *kashruth*? How can we preserve our own lives without jeopardizing those of our brothers?

"Rabbi," I would hear people cry, "Job's suffering was trivial compared to that which is demanded of us today."

Nevertheless, I never heard any of them question the Torah or deny the Almighty's existence.

One night while we were still in our home, a member of our congregation knocked at our door. He had come at the risk of his life. In those days, for a Jew to be found on the street after dark meant certain death.

"Rabbi," he called out in a trembling voice as he entered our house, "you must help me."

My father ushered him into his study and closed the door.

"I have a chance to save my son," he whispered urgently, "I can arrange to have him baptized."

But even as he blurted out these words, he lost control and started to tremble.

"I cannot make this decision alone," he cried, "and that is why I came here. You must help me. Rabbi," he moaned, "what do I do? What alternative do I have? He's my only son." And almost apologetically, he added, "I want him to live."

For the longest time, my father remained silent. Then, in a voice full of anguish, he repeated the man's plea, pronouncing the words slowly, as if each sound was painful to him.

"You want your child to live," he asked, "but tell me, if he is not a Jew, will he live?"

My father's question hung in the air and the room itself seemed to reverberate with it.

"If he's not a Jew, will he live?"

The man turned ashen. "I know, I know," he whispered,

"and I guess I knew it all the time. Please, Rabbi, say no more."

My father got up from his chair, and even as he did so, the tears kept falling into his beard. He reached out for the man and embraced him in his arms.

For a moment, they just stood there, a rabbi and his disciple, bound by an eternal promise to G-d to remain Jews.

The Nazis shut down our synagogues, desecrated our Torah scrolls, burned our Holy Books, and prohibited prayer and study, yet at the risk of our lives we defied them and gathered to worship our G-d. They did everything to degrade us, to sap our spiritual strength and to break our morale, but they could not rob us of our inner spirit.

In the ghettos, in the labor camps, under crushing hardship and brutalizing conditions, in the midst of disease and starvation, we continued to live with honor and dignity. We organized self-help societies to assist the orphans, the widows, and the sick. We established clandestine schools for our children. My mother ran a communal kitchen, while my father converted the ritualarium into a hospital, where to the very last moment, Jewish life was brought into the world (one of the babies born in that makeshift hospital in Szeged is today the Grand Rabbi of a well-known Chassidic community in New York). We may not have had guns with which to battle our enemy, but we had a light from Sinai which illuminated our souls, and of that, no one could deprive us.

My own husband, who was interned in forced labor and concentration camps, never ceased to review the words of the Torah in his mind. Despite his frostbitten feet and gnawing hunger, the teachings of the Bible never left him. He managed to organize a group of young men with whom he studied as he marched and labored on the road. Perhaps never in the annals of mankind were there such scholars as those young men, who in the midst of doom and horror affirmed their love of learning.

Ironically, the most expensive commodity in the camps was not bread nor even cigarettes, but the sacred religious articles of our people: a page from the *siddur*, prayer book, a *mezuzah*, a candle for Sabbath. The Germans would earmark those items for junk, but for a price, it was often possible to salvage them. In our camp we collected two hundred cigarettes in order to buy a *shofar*, ram's horn, for Rosh Hashana.

The news of our purchase spread quickly through the camp underground, and a group of Polish boys from the adjacent compound risked their lives so that they might hear the ancient call of their ancestors. The Germans discovered them and began to beat them mercilessly, but even as the truncheons were falling on their heads, they cried out: "Blessed art Thou, L-rd our G-d, who has commanded us to listen to the sound of the shofar."

I know for a certainty that in the Heavens above, the angels themselves responded, "Amen."

Our tongues may have been parched with thirst, our bodies may have been emaciated with hunger, yet more than for bread and water, we yearned for the prayer book of our fathers. The High Holy Days were upon us, and we could obtain only one *Machzor*, High Holy Day prayer book, for our entire compound.

Who should pray first? Who should pray last? How could one prayer book be passed through so many hands? The rabbis took counsel and decided that we would all learn at least one prayer by heart. But what prayer would it be? Which psalm? Which blessing?

And then they made their decision: *"L'bochen L'vovos"* —"Let us pray to Him who searcheth hearts on the Day of Judgment."

Yes, we invited G-d to come to Bergen-Belsen to search our hearts and determine for Himself whether, despite our pain and suffering, we wavered even one hair's breadth in our faith and love for Him.

Nor were these memories confined to my personal experiences. Other survivors can relate similar tales. Our holidays and festivals were always chosen by the Germans as days to be marked for additional taunting and torture. A friend of mine who was in Auschwitz told me of a group of young girls from Greece, who the Germans decided to send to the gas chambers on Yom Kippur. Cordoned off from the rest of the inmates, the Germans tortured them by offering them food and drink, but it was Yom Kippur, and the girls would not desecrate the day. They refused to eat. In sanctity and holiness, they returned their pure souls to their Creator.

There is an ancient tradition which calls upon the Jew to demonstrate his love of G-d by rising eagerly each and every morning to worship his Creator.

"Do not wait for the morning to awaken you, but let your zeal and fervor for G-d be of such intensity that it awakens the morning and signals daybreak" is the teaching of our sages (*Code of Jewish Law*, Chapter 1).

With my very eyes I saw this happen. In Bergen-Belsen, I saw how mere humans can pierce the darkness and through their devotion bring forth light. At the first sign of dawn, my father would rise and don *tefillin*, phylacteries (small leather boxes encasing handwritten parchment of Biblical passages worn by men on their arms and heads during morning services, which testify that one's mind, heart, and strength are dedicated to G-d). Soon, others would join him and queue up. At great sacrifice and enormous risk, they would wait—not for coffee, nor for bread, but for a moment when they might say *Shema Yisrael* with *tefillin* on their heads.

Those *tefillin* of my father were very special. They had belonged to the *Menuchos Osher*, the Sage of Csenger, my great-grandfather five generations back. When, on the occasion of my father's Bar Mitzva, my grandfather, the rabbi of Nadudvar, presented them to my father, he bestowed upon him a special blessing, that those *tefillin* might remain with him and protect him throughout his life.

Miraculously, during that tragic time, my father's *tefillin* remained untouched, and they accompanied him to these shores, to the United States.

I remember our arrival, and my father gathering us around him.

"Children," my father said, "with the help of the Almighty, we shall build a synagogue, a school, and the little voices which disappeared in the flames will once again sound loud and clear."

And so, the synagogue was built and a *yeshiva* was started with seven children. And the seven became ten, and the ten became one hundred. With each passing day, more children came, and my parents' dream came closer to fulfillment.

Then, one winter day, while my parents were visiting me, the phone rang. It was one of my father's neighbors calling to inform us that the synagogue was engulfed in flames. Some street urchins had entered the building and set the Holy Ark on fire.

It was a long and agonizing ride to the synagogue, and we hardly spoke. We had too many memories, too many fires that we had seen. We couldn't bear to see flames again.

In the darkness, my father kept searching the ruins. We tried to prevail upon him to go home, but he remained adamant and kept sifting through the ashes. Then, in the early hours of the morning, when we were all falling away from exhaustion, he told us that everything would be all right, that now he was ready to go home.

"I have found what I was looking for," he said, and as he

spoke, my father held out his *tefillin,* which he had always kept in the Holy Ark.

The Ark had been enveloped in flames, but miraculously, the *tefillin* survived.

"We shall rebuild," my father said.

In those *tefillin* can be found the story of our nation. In every generation, in every age, and in every country, we have walked into fire, but, by the grace of G-d, we have emerged unscathed.

Obviously, not all of us were able to adhere so tenaciously to the Commandments or retain our beliefs. But there is nothing remarkable about that. In peace as well as in war, there have always been individuals who turned their backs on G-d. What is significant, however, and what must be remembered for all time, is that despite the unspeakable horror, even those among us who were left hopelessly embittered would never have considered conversion or abandoning their faith.

Today, in major capitals of the world, wherever Jews reside, there are neighborhoods dotted with little synagogues that have strange-sounding names such as Satmar, Pupa, Belz, Munkach, Ger, Bobov, Lubavitch, Klausenberg, and even Szeged.

Once they were villages, cities, entire communities, where men and women raised children to sing, to laugh, to be "builders of peace" who worshipped G-d in reverence.

Today they are no more. They were consumed in the flames. But from each place a spark remained, a spark which became a synagogue where the Torah is taught and the Jewish people live on. And *that* is the miracle that should give us all pause—that greater than our personal persecution is the eternity of our people.

After the Holocaust, we, the survivors (and in a sense,

we are all survivors), have a sacred mission to live our lives in such a way that through us, those who perished would once again find life. We are not a nation that believes in memorials of stone. Ours is the awesome task of raising sons and daughters who, imbued with faith, will become *living memorials* for those who are no more.

We must kindle the Sabbath lights, not only for ourselves, but for the millions of mothers who are no longer able to do so. We must study the Torah, not only for ourselves, but for those magnificent young men who were cut down in their youth before they could ever finish singing G-d's Song.

We must pronounce prayers, not only for ourselves, but for the beautiful little children who with their very last breaths sanctified G-d's Name and pronounced a blessing. In the end, that is the only meaningful memorium that we can offer a nation that chose to walk in the flames rather than deny its G-d.

This in no way means that I or our people can ever be at peace with the torment and the unbearable pain that was inflicted on us. My grandfather on my mother's side, Rabbi Tzvi Hirsh Kohn, who survived the Holocaust and saw his community, his congregation, his *yeshiva*, and his family wiped out, never came to terms with the enormity of the suffering.

"When G-d calls me," he would say, "I will arrive with a stick and demand an explanation for the millions of our innocent people who were cast into the crematoria."

But even as my grandfather would wave his big stick, his faith in G-d remained unflinching. He was a righteous man who observed with love the minutia of every Commandment, but at the same time, did not hesitate to do battle for his martyred people. When my grandfather raised his voice in protest, he was following in the tradition of our ancestors.

The patriarch Abraham was the first to demand: "Shall not the Judge of all the earth do justly?" (*Genesis* 18:23).

Moses, Jeremiah, and Job all pleaded to understand why the wicked prosper and the righteous suffer. And Job, in the midst of his anguish, cried out: "Though He slay me, yet I will trust Him, but I will argue my ways before Him" (*Job* 13:15).

Those of our people who today attribute their lack of faith to the Holocaust have never really absorbed the enormity of our suffering. Mass murder, burning, infanticide, psychological degradation and oppression, rape, death marches, pogroms, expulsions, and martyrdom, have, alas, always been our lot.

Centuries before Auschwitz, we learned to weep for our children who were crushed into the pyramids, for our people who were brutally murdered, but throughout, we never denied our G-d or lost our faith. True, in Auschwitz barbarism may have reached hitherto unprecedented heights, and modern technology made the murder of millions rather than thousands possible, but that in no way changed the reality of our tragedy. We are a nation that mourns with the same intensity for the life of one innocent child as for many. To us, each soul is precious, each life is a world unto itself.

I met a man in Montreal. His hands trembled without stop.

"Rebbetzin," he said, "can I have a few minutes of your time? I was told you have a book coming out. I have a little story. Perhaps you would write about it."

I have heard many tales about those days of demonic madness, but I don't think I can ever forget that man's story.

"For two years, I was hiding," he said, "I and my little daughter. She had long golden locks and the most wonderful blue eyes. She was only four.

"And then, one day, someone informed on us, and they came to flush us out. I grabbed my little girl in my arms and started to run with them close behind. My little girl was smart. She understood what was happening.

" 'Daddy, daddy,' she whispered, 'you run and leave me here. You will never make it if you have to carry me, but alone you will have a chance.'

"Hush, little one," I said, and I kept running, holding on to her tightly. But they caught up to us, and they shot my beautiful little girl in my arms."

I looked at the man, but I could see only his trembling, outstretched hands.

Yes, we are a nation to whom every soul is sacred. The death of one little girl can leave a father's hands forever trembling and a nation's heart forever scarred.

Had the world shared with us this regard for life, had they rebelled at the shedding of our Jewish blood, Hitler could have been stopped before the world was engulfed in conflagration. But with the advent of the Holocaust, life became cheap.

For the first time in history, human beings were processed into matter. Skins were fashioned into lampshades, bones ground into fertilizer, bodies processed into soap. The entire structure of traditional Western values was obliterated.

For centuries, mankind nurtured the illusion that through education and culture a man could become civilized and refined, but the Holocaust came to mock all these pretensions. Suddenly, it became possible to spend a day at the human slaughterhouse torturing and killing millions, and then return home to graciously entertain guests to the strains of *"Eine Kleine Nachtmusik."*

The Nazis proved that a man could be of impeccable breeding, a master of science and technology, and yet be lower than the beasts.

The Holocaust testifies that education and culture are worthless, that universities and social institutions cannot transform a man into a decent human being, and that in the final analysis, only knowledge that is based on the Word of G-d can humanize.

It is this knowledge of G-d that we as a nation were commissioned to uphold through our Covenant, and for its sake we were prepared to undergo even the ultimate sacrifice.

The patriarch Abraham and his son were the first to accept this yoke of the Covenant which G-d warned would entail a legacy of suffering and exile.

"And G-d said unto Abraham, 'Know for a surety that thy seed shall be a stranger in a land that is not theirs, and shall serve there, and they shall be afflicted. . . .'" (*Genesis* 15:13).

This prophecy of our first exile was followed by prophecies that would see us scattered throughout the four corners of the earth. And how could it be otherwise? How else could we fulfill our mission and bear witness to the Word of G-d?

In the midst of every nation, we became a minority that refused to allow itself to be absorbed, that stubbornly clung to its heritage, and even at pain of death refused to compromise its faith.

And so, with Bible in hand, we surged forth as a spiritual army, and if in fulfilling our task we had to encounter the gas chambers, even there we raised our voices and declared, "*Ani ma'amin*—I believe."

Our father Abraham taught us well.

Our Bible, our prayer book, all served to imprint this legacy of faith and martyrdom on our souls. On every High Holy Day, when the cantor would begin to chant the prayer of the Ten Holy Martyrs who were savagely tortured to death by the Romans, I would see the history of our people unfold before my eyes, and as I would feel the terrible weight of their suffering, my prayer book would become drenched with tears.

It is written that the very angels in the Heavens above

could not bear to witness the agony of those saintly martyrs.

"Is this then the reward of the righteous? Is this then the Torah?" they asked.

To which a Heavenly Voice replied, "If I hear another sound, I shall surely recall the world into nothingness."

In order for humanity to survive, there must be those who are ready to sacrifice for truth and righteousness, who, in their determination to disseminate the Word of G-d are even willing to undergo the ultimate test. The angels could not bear to witness the suffering that this entailed, but the Ten Holy Martyrs accepted their fate, for greater than their pain was their love of G-d, and with their last breaths they pronounced the *Shema* (our declaration of faith in the Oneness of G-d).

The Romans may have brutally tortured and murdered them, but their *Shema* spanned the centuries. I heard it behind the barbed wire, at the gates of the gas chambers, and in the flames of the crematoria.

The Nazis, even as the Romans, were not content to merely take our people to the slaughter. More than our individual deaths, they sought the obliteration of our faith. With ferocity they pounced upon our Law, plundered and burned our Torahs, mutilated our Holy Books, and took pleasure in desecrating that which we held sacred.

When, centuries ago, the Romans took our sages to be martyred, they enveloped them in the Holy Scrolls and immolated them. But they failed to realize that the flames could consume only the parchment—the letters of the Torah escaped, and together with the souls of the martyrs ascended Heavenward. To this very day, these letters hover in the skies. I saw them above the chimneys and I know they accompanied the holy innocent souls to the Throne of G-d.

It was 1939 when the madman, Hitler, unleashed his satanic hatred upon mankind, and once again the call went forth to us to envelop ourselves in the Holy Scrolls of the

Torah. And through the pages of our Bible, our history, and our prayer book, we had a glimpse, a perception, of what was happening to us. Our past and our present merged.

Av Harachamim is the prayer that we recite every Sabbath: "May the Father of Mercies who dwelleth on high, in His mighty compassion remember those loving, upright, and blameless souls, the holy congregations who laid down their lives for the sanctification of the Divine Name, who were lovely and pleasant in their lives, and who in their deaths were not separated."

This prayer was composed in 1096 after the first Crusaders slaughtered the Jewish communities of the Rhineland, but it could just as easily have been written in 1939 in Germany, Poland, Lithuania, Russia, Rumania, Greece, Czechoslovakia, France, Italy, Yugoslavia, and in my town—Szeged, Hungary.

It was 1939, and I was destined to see the pages of my history book come alive in fire. I was hurt, I was wounded, I moaned and I wept, but never did I lose sight of that Covenant sealed at Sinai—to be a witness to the Word of G-d.

Yet there were others who did not fare as well, whose suffering left them permanently crippled. They were the ones who had shed their Jewishness, who staked their faith in twentieth-century humanism, who were convinced that if only we, the Jewish people, would allow ourselves to be integrated into society, anti-Semitism would cease to exist.

Then, suddenly, without warning, the balloon burst. All their illusions about culture, education, humanity, the brotherhood of man, Christian love and charity, came crashing down on their heads. Hitler not only derided their adulation of culture, but expelled them from all those places that they had come to hold sacred: the university, the science lab, society, and life itself.

Overnight, the beliefs which they had cherished, the values for which they had sacrificed, collapsed. But perhaps most painful of all was the realization that this madman was the product of their world, the world that they had admired and helped create—sophisticated enlightened Germany. Germany, where the Jew had bartered his Torah values for twentieth-century mores, where Herr Doktor had become the new sage, where the *yarmulke* and the *tallis* had been discarded, where conversion and intermarriage had reached unprecedented heights, and where the Jew was willing to deny his faith in order to become accepted. It was from here that the horror spilled forth.

Ironically, throughout our long history, our tormentors always gave us a choice: Convert or be killed—and we never had any doubts as to what our answer must be. But with the advent of twentieth-century humanism, all that changed, and for the first time there were those among us who would not have passed the ultimate test, who in their desire to assimilate had renounced their Jewishness, and it was precisely at that moment that Hitler closed the door and there was no longer a choice.

The country that prided itself on its humanism denied basic human rights to the Jew, and the land became an inferno from which there was no escape.

There was a woman in an adjacent camp, who, prior to the war had been among the social elite. Pathetically, she kept telling everyone who would listen that it was all a mistake, that she was not a Jew at all, that she never even had Jewish friends, but despite her protestations, the Nazis marked her for the gas chambers.

A friend of mine told me that imprisoned with him in Auschwitz was an SS officer. A thorough check into his family tree revealed traces of Jewish blood. Overnight, despite the SS symbol tattooed in his armpit, he became vermin to be exterminated.

These rootless souls were perhaps the most pathetic figures of the Holocaust. They were neither fish nor fowl, and tragically, it was Hitler who had to remind them of their Jewishness.

Those of us who were blessed with insight into our Bible and our history were better able to cope, but I must concede that nothing could have prepared us for the naked bestiality of the Nazis.

I recall when, prior to our deportation, news filtered back to us that our people were being gassed by the millions, burned in ovens, and processed into soap. We convinced ourselves that such rumors could only be the hallucinations of madmen. After all, who in his right mind could conceive of such inhumanity?

The Germans also did their share to dissuade us from believing these ghoulish tales. Upon occupation, their first order of business was to reassure us that we would not be harmed. We had only to adhere to some simple regulations: Register, get working papers, and cooperate. Those who refused to obey were severely punished, and the Germans knew exactly where we Jews were most vulnerable. They tormented us by harassing our families, by torturing our children and our elderly, and by killing hundreds, if not thousands, in reprisal for any act of rebellion. Once they made an arrest, their cruelty became satanic. They made us witness the torture of those who had to die a thousand and one deaths.

By the time we arrived in the concentration camps, the ghettos and the forced labor battalions had left their mark. We were broken and emaciated, ravaged by disease, and whatever strength we had left had been crushed in the cattle cars.

I write all this because I could never bear the glib remarks of those who demand to know why we went like sheep to the slaughter. Pray, with what should we have fought? We had no arms, we had no army. We had no government, and we were trapped in enemy territory. And yet I doubt very much if ever in the annals of mankind there was such evidence of valor as was demonstrated by our people, not only in the Warsaw Ghetto, but in ghettos and concentration camps throughout Europe.

The question which must be asked after the Holocaust is not why we did not fight, but how it was possible that we did rebel; how we, a nation of walking skeletons, dared to battle Goliath, how our sons and daughters found the courage to become burning torches and with their bare hands hold back the tanks of the enemy.

And so, the question is not why we did not fight, but why the nations did nothing.

In the very beginning, the gates of Europe were open. Hitler was committed to making Europe *Judenrein*, free of Jews. He allowed us to leave, but there was no place that would accept us. The stories of our futile attempts to save ourselves and our children are well-documented and can fill volumes.

In 1939, the *St. Louis* left Hamburg with 930 of our people on board. They were among the select privileged few who had a place to go. They all had Cuban visas in their possession, but before they ever reached the shores of Havana, the Cuban government rescinded their papers. Most of these refugees also held United States immigration quota numbers which would have entitled them to enter the United States at some future date, but despite all that, the American government refused to grant them even temporary sanctuary.

The Germans got the message loud and clear. There would be no interference in the extermination of Jews.

The stories go on: In 1941, there was the *Sturma*. The vessel was nothing more than a ramshackle cattle boat, but our people were desperate and willing to take any risk to save themselves. Seven hundred and sixty-nine of them crammed onto the deck in a last-ditch attempt to reach Palestine. The conditions on board were abominable, but no one complained, and the miracle occurred—they reached Turkey.

The Turkish officials would not allow them to disembark. Jewish Agency representatives from Palestine tried valiantly to save at least the children on board, but that, too, was denied. For ten weeks, the crippled ship lay in the waters of the Bosphorus, until the Turks insisted that it leave. Eighty Turkish policemen forced their way on board and tugged the *Sturma* into the Black Sea, and there, the *Sturma*, together with the six million, disappeared.

To have reached freedom, to have been so close to a new life, and then to be cast into the sea in full view of the entire civilized world is perhaps even more ghastly than to be forced at gunpoint into the crematoria.

And yet, they ask us why we did not fight.

Toward the end of the war, there was a brief moment when the cattle cars going to the death camps finally did come to a halt. The Germans were encountering serious setbacks on all fronts. They were in desperate need of supplies, and overnight, we, the Jewish people, became a marketable commodity. Adolf Eichmann called in the president of the Hungarian Jewish community and actually put us up for sale. His proposal was brutal and calculating: "Goods for blood, blood for goods. You can take them from any country you like, wherever you can find them—from Hungary, Poland, the Eastern Provinces, from Terezin, from Auschwitz, wherever you want. Whom do you wish to save? Men who can beget children? Women who can bear them? Old people? Children? Sit down and talk. If you tell me that my offer has been accepted, I will close Auschwitz and bring ten percent of the promised million to the frontier. You can take away a hundred thousand Jews, and afterward bring a thousand trucks. We'll go on like that—a thousand trucks for every hundred thousand Jews."

At the time, we weren't privy to the details of this proposal, but the news did filter back to us that something was in the offing. The Germans were willing to negotiate, but there were no takers. No one was interested in buying Jews. It was evident that the freedom-loving nations were more perturbed at the prospect of Jews infiltrating their shores than of seeing us marched to the gas chambers. Moreover, the Allies had detailed information about our fate, but they never acted. We begged that they at least bomb the railroad tracks leading to Auschwitz, but even that they did not do. Until the very last moment, the ovens worked overtime.

And yet they ask, "Why?" Why didn't we fight? And where was our G-d?

I have often wondered how man can have no shame, how he does not shudder at the sight of his bloody hands, how he is not revolted at his own hypocrisy.

What happened to the forces of education and culture? Why did the laws of morality not prevent the defilement of humanity? Why did twentieth-century man fail to be worthy of the title "man"?

What is man? Is he a victim, or is he free? Is he accountable for his deeds, or is he a robot? Is he a puppet to be manipulated, or a being endowed with freedom of choice?

Should we decide that man is a victim and thereby absolve him of responsibility for the Holocaust, then we must extend this same courtesy to every criminal. The murderer, the thief, the mugger, could all plead innocent and blame G-d for their crimes. On the other hand, if we believe that man must be held accountable for his deeds, we must also indict him for the atrocities of the Holocaust. One thing is certain, we cannot have it both ways. We cannot declare man a free, intelligent being, and then proceed to attribute the horrors that are of his making to G-d.

The Bible teaches us that man has been endowed with freedom of choice. "There is blessing, there is curse, there is life, and there is death, and you shall choose life" (*Deuteronomy* 30:19) is G-d's admonition. The emphasis is on the word "choose," for it is that choice which elevates man above the beast and renders him a human being.

The Nazis had that choice and they opted for unbridled bestiality.

The nations of the world had that choice, and they opted for complicity through silence.

And G-d Himself (so to speak) had a choice—to annihilate man, or to await his repentance. Had He opted for the destruction of evil, He would have had to bring an end to the world as we know it today and negate the freedom of choice on which human life is based.

"As I live, saith the L-rd G-d, I have no pleasure in the death of the wicked, but that the wicked turn from his way and live" (*Ezekiel* 33:11).

But that turning point, that change of heart, cannot be brought about by G-d. It is only man who can make it happen, and tragically, in the process, the innocent will be hurt.

This in no way implies that G-d is unconcerned with our fate. On the contrary, He is always there, waiting for man to repent and mend his ways. That waiting is G-d's suffering, which forces Him to veil His Countenance, to appear as if He is in hiding.

More than anything else, G-d yearns to be found, but He cannot find *us*. It is we who must find *Him,* for it is through that quest that we can rise above the beast, become better people, and be worthy of the spirit that He instilled within us.

In order to allow the world to function, G-d must curb His infinite power. He can command, teach, guide, and even punish, but He cannot impose His will on us without rendering us robots, without denying us that purification of soul which results from a repentant heart.

When Cain, the first murderer, killed his brother, Abel, G-d hoped to evoke feelings of contrition in him.

"Where is your brother Abel?" G-d asked. "His blood crieth out to Me from the earth . . ." (*Genesis* 4:9, 10).

But Cain remained obdurate, and shamelessly proclaimed: "Am I my brother's keeper?" (*Genesis*, 4:9).

And today, thousands of years later, nothing has changed. In vain did G-d command, "Thou shalt not kill" (*Exodus* 20:13). In vain did He warn that, yes, we are not only our brother's keeper, but more, we dare not stand idly by while his life is in jeopardy (*Leviticus* 19:16).

Man continues to defile his freedom of choice and refuses to heed the Voice of G-d.

But even G-d's endurance has measure, and although He must restrain His infinite strength, there is a Covenant that must be maintained upon which the world stands. That Covenant demands that we, the Jewish people, remain His witness. And who else can bear witness if not a nation that emerged from the flames? Who else, if not a nation that is a miniscule minority in a sea of hostility, a nation that is driven from country to country and does not lose its identity, a nation that is cast into the crematoria and yet remains alive, a nation that by its existence testifies that: "Not by might nor by power, but by My spirit, sayeth the L-rd," that nation becomes a witness to the Holy Name of G-d (*Zechariah* 4:6).

And so, throughout those days of darkness, I knew beyond all doubt that G-d would never totally abandon us, that although the entire world had turned against us, we would overcome, for in the final analysis, it is in our survival as a nation that G-d's presence is manifest.

I may have been standing in the mud of Bergen-Belsen,

but alongside of me I felt the presence of my brothers and sisters who lived thousands of years before me—babies who were cast into the Nile by Pharaoh, children who were massacred by the Syrians, the Romans, the Greeks; sons and daughters who were tortured by the Crusaders, brothers and sisters who chose the pyres of the Inquisition over renunciation of their faith. They all stood with me, and they taught me a song, *"Ani ma'amin,* I believe."

thirteen

&

THE CHALLENGE

THE NIGHTS IN BERGEN-BELSEN were very long. The scurrying of rats, the horrible odors, the wailing and crying kept me awake. I would close my eyes and try to escape by recalling stories from the Bible, stories of our sages, stories of Jerusalem.

There was one particular tale that I loved the most. It was about Rabbi Akiva, one of the Ten Holy Martyrs. I felt that I knew him, for he also saw flames. He saw the fall of Jerusalem, the ruin of our sacred Temple, the slaughter of our beautiful children, and yet he never lost hope.

It is written that at the time of the destruction of our Holy Temple, Rabbi Akiva and the sages of Israel were walking on the streets of Jerusalem. As they came to the Temple Mount, they beheld a devastating sight. There, where the sanctuary had once stood in majesty and splendor, were only ruins, and wild animals roamed about.

The sages of Israel broke down and wept.

"Woe is us," they wailed, "that we have been destined to see this with our own eyes."

But it is related that Rabbi Akiva did not weep. Instead he smiled.

"How can you smile at such a time?" his colleagues asked, shocked.

"I smile," Rabbi Akiva answered, "because today I have seen the fulfillment of prophecy, for the same prophet who

227

foretold the destruction also foretold that the Temple shall be rebuilt. The same prophet who prophesied our exile also prophesied that we shall return to Jerusalem in joy. And so I smile, for now that the first part of our prophecy has come to pass, the second part will surely come to be."

"Akiva," the sages declared, "you have comforted us."

And almost two thousand years later, in Bergen-Belsen, Rabbi Akiva comforted me as well.

"This too shall pass," I would tell myself, for this hell on earth was just the first part of the prophecy, and we would yet come to Jerusalem, where the sun always shone, where no one ever went hungry, where, my mother assured me, candy bars actually grew on trees, and birds sang the psalms of King David.

Lying there on my bunk, I could actually feel and taste Jerusalem. But that my fantasies would one day become reality, that we who were forced to descend into the abyss of hell would actually behold the light of Jerusalem, that we, the dead bones, would come to life even as Ezekiel prophesied, was more than I could have hoped for.

> And the L-rd set me down in the valley,
>   and it was full of bones . . .
> Then He said unto me, Son of man,
>   these bones are the whole House of Israel . . .
> Thus saith the L-rd, G-d.
> Behold, I will open up your graves, O my people
> And I will bring you into the land of Israel.
> And you shall know that I am the L-rd. . . .
>   (*Ezekiel* 37:1, 11–13)

Yes, we who were marked for genocide, who saw millions of our little ones perish in the flames, precisely at the moment when we thought we could no longer go on, were vindicated by Rabbi Akiva's smile.

There is no precedent in the annals of mankind for our

miraculous return. Never has a people risen from the grave. Never has a nation returned to its land after two thousand years, and yet we saw it with our very eyes. It was not a vision, it was not a dream. Israel emerged from the ancient past into the twentieth century. Prophecy was fulfilled.

And so it was that even as we were liberated, all our hopes centered around Jerusalem. Israel became the focus of our existence, and more than anything else, we were determined to go there. But a cruel British quota system barred us from reaching her shores. Nevertheless, we resolved to hold out, and patiently waited in Switzerland for our visas.

But as the weeks became months, and the months dragged into years (1945–47), our situation became more and more intolerable. For some inexplicable reason, the administrators of refugee camps in Switzerland had split up our family. My parents were in a D.P. camp in Caux, my brother was detained in Engelberg (German Switzerland), and I was sent to Bex (near Montreux). This separation was sheer torment. Night after night, I would go to bed in a state of abject terror. In the darkness of my room, I saw Nazis everywhere. The chairs, the table, all became Gestapo agents. I wanted to shriek, but my voice choked in my throat, and so I just lay in a pool of sweat, waiting for morning, crying silently for my parents.

As time passed and most of the children in our school were resettled, my suffering became more acute. I was left without a roommate. There was no one with whom I could exchange a word, no one to give me reassurance when the horrible nightmares returned. When my father came to visit, I confided my fears to him. For the longest time, he rocked me in his arms, and then resolutely declared: "Your aunt in New York has sent us visas. We shall leave for America on the first available ship and live like a family again."

But even as we adjusted to our new life in New York, our

hearts remained linked to the Holy City. Three times a day, morning, noon and evening, we recalled Jerusalem. At the conclusion of each meal, in the midst of every celebration, and in moments of grief, we always recalled Jerusalem. We swore that our tongues would cleave to our palates and our right hands wither, before we ever forget Jerusalem (*Psalm 127:5–6*).

In 1948, as the new State of Israel was officially declared, a sense of urgency took hold of my life. I would come home from school, bolt down my dinner, and dash on my way. There were meetings, rallies, fundraisers. There was work to be done. My English still bore traces of my European past, and I spoke with a heavy accent, but this did not deter me from speaking on behalf of Israel, and I made a silent pledge that as soon as I finished high school, I would find my way there.

Even as I laid my plans, I realized that there would be many hurdles to overcome, not the least of which would be leaving my parents. We were a family of survivors. To us, each and every day was a special gift from G-d, and the thought of separation was unbearably painful. Yet I knew that I would have to go, and I also knew that my parents would understand and support me in getting there.

It was 1953 when I set sail. My route took me from New York to Marseilles, where I boarded an Israeli ship bound for Haifa. I will never forget that day in Marseilles when I first beheld the Star of David proudly blowing in the breeze. To have stood at the threshold of the gas chambers and now to board an Israeli vessel with Jewish officers was the stuff of which my dreams had been made in Bergen-Belsen.

My first glimpse of the shores of *Eretz Yisrael* (the Land of Israel) came with the dawn. My heart felt as if it would burst, and tears kept flowing from my eyes. As the sun kissed the mountain tops, the words of David reverberated in my mind:

As the mountains surround Jerusalem, so the L-rd
encompasses His people, from this time forth, for-
evermore . . .

(*Psalm 125:2*)

In this land, I felt I was actually enveloped by G-d. Here,
Abraham, David, the prophets, the sages, lifted prayers and
carried them straight to the Throne of the Creator. Yes, this
land was different, for "the eyes of the L-rd our G-d are upon
this land from the beginning of the year to the end of the
year" (*Deuteronomy* 11:12).

I set foot on the holy ground, bowed deep to kiss its soil,
and intoned the traditional prayer which every Jew pronounces upon arriving in Israel: "Blessed art Thou, O L-rd
our G-d, King of the universe, who has enabled us to reach
this day."

Overcome by the awesomeness of the moment, I was
oblivious to my surroundings, but all too soon the twentieth
century came crashing down on my head. Customs, baggage,
porters, taxis. There was much shouting and pushing, and
the gap between vision and reality jarred, but only for a
moment. I quickly realized that this, too, was a blessing.
Today we have a port, I said to myself; today we have the
normal hustle and bustle of a metropolis. I was in Israel, and
nothing could dampen my spirits.

I had prepared myself for hard work and rugged living
conditions, and in a sense I was even looking forward to the
sacrifice that I knew life in Israel demanded of each and
every one. What caught me unawares was that not everyone
was an idealist, not that I was so naive as to imagine that
people actually went to work singing and dancing horas. But
neither did I anticipate cynicism and open hostility toward
religion.

For the first time, I became frightened, for I knew that if
we had survived the centuries, it was only because there was
a greater law which dictated our existence, and that law

came from G-d Himself. But the agnostics that I met repudiated these eternal laws. They believed that the establishment of the State rendered the Torah obsolete, that merely by living in the land they could fulfill their Jewishness and discard our timeless heritage. They scoffed at the idea that the return to the land was made possible only so that we might fulfill our prophetic destiny: "For out of Zion shall go forth Torah, and the Word of G-d from Jerusalem" (*Isaiah* 2:3).

There is a mystical component to our existence. We are a Torah nation, destined to be G-d's witness here on earth, to dwell alone in sanctity.

To thee and to thy seed will I give this land forever.
(*Genesis* 13:15)

Slowly, I began to understand that patience and fortitude would be required, that even as we had to cultivate our land, so we would have to regenerate our hearts. After all, it was after two thousand years of dispersion that we had come home, two thousand years during which we traversed the four corners of the world, two thousand years of torture and humiliation, two thousand years during which we were divided by language, civilization, and culture, and overnight, the creation of the State demanded that we become one. Among us were Jews from the cosmopolitan cities of Paris, London and New York, as well as from far away lands like Yemen, Iraq, and Kurdistan, countries that were cut off from the technological revolution of the twentieth century. We were worlds apart, but suddenly, we were all living side by side.

Moses had forty years to prepare our ancestors to enter the land, to forge them into a nation. But our return came with the swiftness of the "wink of an eye." We were a wounded people; one third of our sons and daughters had been slaughtered, yet despite it all, we reclaimed our land, built cities, organized a government and molded an army. We, who for two thousand years were never allowed to defend ourselves, never permitted to hold a weapon in our hands, who only yesterday were fuel for the crematoria, overnight took on the might of David and defeated Goliath.

The very fact that we were able to accomplish all this was a sign that G-d Himself was leading us. To be sure, many problems remained, but we were a nation of miracles, and never for a moment did I doubt that we would make it.

I threw myself into my new life. I studied, worked, and on my days off I traversed the length and breadth of the land. I never tired of exploring, and wondrously, there was always something new to discover. It was a paradox: The land was miniscule, and yet its depth was infinite. Every speck of dust was laden with history; the air was dense with sanctity. Here, the Bible came alive; here the prophets, the sages, the martyrs of every age were to be found. It was intoxicating. I was actually able to walk where my ancestors had passed, to pray at the graves of my forefathers, to stand in the valley where David defeated Goliath, the mountains where Elijah unmasked the priests of Baal and sanctified the Name of G-d. I was in the land of the Bible. I was home.

But perhaps most exciting of all was to behold the miracle of the land. The highways built in the deserts; the cities and villages mushrooming overnight; the gardens and forests blooming in soil that had long been eroded and dead. It was prophecy come alive.

> I will restore the fortune of My people, Israel,
>> and they shall rebuild the ruined cities and inhabit them.
> They shall plant vineyards and drink their wine
>> and they shall plant gardens and eat their fruit.

> I will plant them upon their land and they shall never
> again be plucked out of the land which I have given
> them saith the L-rd.
>
> > (*Amos* 9:14–15)

For two thousand years, the land remained desolate and
barren, her rich soil infested with malaria swamps, her cities
in ruins. Throughout this period, many nations tried to conquer her, to rebuild her waste places, to bring forth her fruit,
but none succeeded. G-d Himself had made a promise that
the land would await our homecoming and only upon our
return would the trees once again sing in the forest.

And now, wherever I went, I saw lush green fields, and I
never ceased to marvel at the miracle of a dormant land
coming to life again.

But it was not only the miraculous rebirth of our land
that left me breathless. Equally exhilarating was the wonder of the homecoming of our people, the ingathering of
the exiles.

> Fear not My people, Israel, for I am with thee.
> I will bring thy seed from the east, and gather them
> > from the west,
> I will say to the north "give up," and to the south "keep
> > not back."
> Bring My sons from far, and My daughters from the
> > ends of the earth.
>
> > (*Isaiah* 43:5,6)

For centuries, the Jews of Yemen had lived in isolation,
cut off from Western civilization. They led a simple, primitive existence. They had no familiarity with modern technology, knowledge of the Holocaust, or any of the events that
befell us. Then, suddenly, news filtered back to them that
Israel was reborn, and they immediately responded by leaving their homes and walking in the direction of Jerusalem.
How they would get there, they did not know, but they were

convinced that G-d would show them the way. En route, they were robbed and taunted, but no matter, they kept walking toward Jerusalem. Thousands upon thousands of them converged upon Aden, where the young Israeli government made provisions to fly them home in what was fondly dubbed, "Operation Magic Carpet."

I became fast friends with a Yemenite girl. We were civilizations apart, and yet we had everything in common. We were Jews who had returned home after two thousand years. I would sit spellbound while she related stories of her family, and she, in turn, was fascinated by my stories of the Holocaust.

In Yemen, they had never seen a radio, a car, or a train, and yet without hesitation, they boarded the planes.

"Weren't you afraid to fly?" I asked.

"Of course not," she laughed. "Didn't G-d Himself promise to fly us on wings of eagles to our land?"

I think it was this genuine faith of the Yemenite community, coupled with their natural warmth and love, that especially endeared them to my heart. I decided that I would find my career in teaching their children, but before I could realize my plan, I fell gravely ill and was hospitalized in Jerusalem.

When news of my illness reached my parents, they became terribly concerned and made arrangements for my recuperation in the States. Thus, a new chapter in my life unfolded.

Not too long after my return, I married my fifth cousin, who also came to the U.S. in 1947. The Holocaust left him orphaned, and over the years he had become very much a part of our family. It was only after my return from Israel, however, that we realized that our relationship could develop into something more than one between cousins. Together, we decided to continue to labor on behalf of our people. But the more involved we became in Jewish life, the more we realized that the return of our people to Israel would have to be complemented by a return to our heritage, for if Israel is to survive, then the Kevins, the Bobbys, the Harolds, the Lauries, and the Phils would have to become total Jews again.

But all our efforts in reclaiming our people could not accomplish that which the year 1967 brought about, when in six lightning days Jerusalem was reunited with her children.

It was not by coincidence that the liberation of David's city signaled a Jewish awakening, for Jerusalem had been designated to bear witness together with us. Therefore, every aspect of her redemption had to be miraculous, beyond logic, so that even the blind might see and the deaf might hear the Word of G-d.

Never before were the odds so heavily weighted against us, never before was our defeat so imminent. The combined Arab forces swore to exterminate us. There was absolutely no one to come to our defense, and once again the world remained silent.

But how could it be otherwise, for how else could G-d's Name be sanctified? How else could the Holy City bear witness with us?

As the news from Jerusalem became ever more menacing, our response also became more heroic. Jerusalem was a city built on the love of the brothers, and therefore we perceived that it could be redeemed only through our unqualified love.

It was June, 1967, and we, the nation that had always been splintered, polarized, divided, and fragmented, became one. Overnight, all our differences dissipated. The petty bickering that usually marks our community life was suspended. Our love for Jerusalem neutralized all jealousies, overrode all politics. In every synagogue, our people gathered to pray. Lines formed in front of every Israeli embassy, volunteers by the thousands offered their resources, their strength, their very lives, and in an unprecedented act of unity, we of the American Jewish community put aside all our differences. It was not the Orthodox, the Conservative, or the Reform who went to Washington to plead on behalf of the Holy City, but all of us as one.

And in Israel itself, the nation responded above and beyond the call of duty. Every adult was at the front. School children took over the running of social services, and even those who were in distant lands returned home to battle on behalf of Jerusalem.

My brother-in-law, who was the Rabbi of a small town near Tel Aviv, wrote about one of his students, a boy of eighteen who at the outbreak of the war was recuperating from a broken leg. He couldn't bear the thought of staying home while his brethren were at the front, and so, despite his pain, he removed his cast and joined his unit. Although he was in agony, he fought on, and no one ever knew of his handicap.

There was yet another family in his congregation. They had come from Yemen with eight sons, and all eight were in the thick of battle. Their mother, beside herself with worry, consulted a sage and begged that he advise her where she might best pray for the safe return of her children.

"At which grave should I knock? Who should I awaken from slumber? Who will be the righteous messenger to carry my plea to G-d's Throne?" she wondered.

The sage pondered her question for a while, and then instructed her not to pray at any grave, but to go home and await her children.

"Know, my dear woman," he told her, "the graves of the holy souls are empty. They are all at the front battling alongside your sons, watching over them. Be assured that they will bring them home in safety."

Yes, this war was different. The patriarchs, the prophets, the martyrs of all ages converged upon the battlefield, and at their sight tens of thousands of the enemy fled.

"And you shall chase your enemies and they shall fall before you. Five of you shall chase one hundred, and one hundred of you shall chase ten thousand, and your enemy shall fall before you" (*Leviticus* 26:7, 8).

And was it not so? Did we not see it with our very eyes? Did not five Israeli soldiers chase one hundred? And did not the hundreds chase the thousands? For those who went forth to liberate Jerusalem were not simply soldiers, but they were David, Gideon, Joshua, Samson, and the Maccabbees, coming to life in the twentieth century.

The sons of David broke through the ancient gates, bullets whizzed over their heads, fire blazed on every side, but nothing could hold them back. They had a rendezvous with destiny, to fulfill G-d's promise. Quick as lightning, they made their way through the serpentine alleyways, never pausing to catch their breaths until they came upon that sacred place: the Western Wall, the only remnant of the Holy Temple, which G-d declared would forever wait for their homecoming.

And throughout the long and torturous centuries, the Wall waited. No one could console her, no one could give her comfort. It was only her children whom she wanted. Then, suddenly, without warning, we were embracing her, washing her with our tears, kissing her with our lips, caressing her with our prayers and love. And as we sounded the shofar, the ancient call of our fathers, the reverberations were felt in every land. We, the Jewish people, had come home. From Auschwitz to Jerusalem, a two-thousand-year-old promise had been kept; Rabbi Akiva's smile had been vindicated.

The effect was magical. Our people became spiritually rejuvenated. Even those who never believed, who were hardened cynics, felt something in their hearts. The Wall called them, and despite themselves they had to respond, to touch its stones, to place a note with a prayer in its crevices, to stand for a moment in its presence, to pour out their hearts and even cry.

My husband and I made a decision. We knew that no matter what, we, too, had to be there, and so we took our four small children and traveled to Jerusalem. The city was congested with people, there wasn't a hotel room to be had. For a moment, I panicked, but then my husband reminded me of the teaching of our Talmud: In Jerusalem, no one ever complained of discomfort, in the City of G-d every man had a place, everyone was welcome.

It was Friday, *erev Shabbat*, when we arrived, and there was no time to be lost. The Queen Sabbath was quickly approaching and the entire city was readying herself for the arrival of the royal guest. Everywhere, stores were closing and public transportation was coming to a halt. As the siren was sounded, a stillness descended on the Holy City.

The Queen Sabbath had arrived, and in her honor candles were kindled in every home, blessings were recited, and songs were sung. Suddenly, scores of people spilled into the streets. They came from every direction: young and old, men and women, Israelis and tourists, students and soldiers, pious Chassidim in long black coats and westernized Jews in business suits. They came from the four corners of the world. They spoke in many tongues, espoused many ideas, and wondrously, they all merged into one. All of them were rushing, running to the same place, to the Wall.

We, too, melted into the crowd. We didn't know our way, but we just followed the others. This was the land of our fathers. The prophets and sages of Israel would show us the way. My heart beat faster, and I clutched my children's hands. I saw tears in my husband's eyes. We were in Jerusalem.

All around us, people were singing, "Come let us greet the Sabbath Queen." Even the trees seemed to murmur psalms. Our steps took on momentum. That my family and I were actually here, walking in the midst of this great multitude to the *Kotel*, to the Wall, was too marvelous to comprehend.

We made our way through the dark alleyways. My son tugged at my sleeve. "*Ema*," he asked, "how did our soldiers do it? How did they liberate the city? How did they get through these gates, these alleys?"

"Jerusalem's time had come," I answered, "and G-d Himself opened the gates."

Suddenly, without warning, the Wall was upon us, more majestic than I could ever have imagined. She greeted us in mysterious splendor and took hold of our hearts. We stood as if in a trance—my husband, my children, and I. We could not speak. There were only tears. For two thousand years, we had waited for this moment. Our ancestors had prayed for this day. What they would not have given to stand here, even for a fleeting second, and yet they were denied the privilege. How strange that we who were unworthy, we who were wanting in faith, were the ones to stand here in the presence of sanctity. How, I wondered, could we prove ourselves worthy? How dare we approach this holy place?

I looked up at the Heavens and searched for my grandfather. Surely the angels had gathered his ashes from Auschwitz and brought them as an offering to this very spot.

"*Zeide, zeide*," I cried into the night, "please walk with me, for here I cannot stand alone."

We made our way through the crowds, and now we were actually able to touch the ancient stones. All around us people were praying, and our voices became one with theirs. I looked up at the Wall and I saw countless papers protruding from the crevices. They were letters to the Almighty G-d written by His children, beseeching Him to grant salvation, peace, and strength. There were thousands upon thousands of these requests, but miraculously, there was room for mine, too, for this was Jerusalem. Here, no one lacked space, here, every heart found a place.

I buried my face in the Wall. The coolness of the stones soothed me. I poured out my soul. A gentle breeze was in the air and a wonderful serenity descended upon me. I looked up at the foliage sprouting from the crevices. Strange, I thought to myself, how these little flowers grow without being watered. But then I saw the people around me, and I understood from whence these flowers received their nourishment. They were watered by the tears of a nation that had been waiting for two thousand years.

Here, the martyrs of all ages gather. Here, they come to greet their children. Here, the past and the present merge. Here, it is written, the Spirit of G-d shall forever hover.

It grew late, and on our way back my husband told my children of King David's magical harp.

It is said that night after night, when David, King of Israel, retired to his chambers, he would place his harp upon his window sill, and when in the stillness of the night the winds of Jerusalem would start to blow, the harp of David would respond with a sweet, soft tune: "Awake, O King," it would call, "arise and sing praises to your G-d."

And when David would hear the call of the harp, he would rise from his bed and create yet another psalm, and to this very day, at midnight at the Wall, as the winds of Jerusalem blow, there are those who can hear the harp of David sing its sweet song.

"*Abba*," my children asked, "do you think that we could come back to the Wall at midnight? Perhaps, if we stand here, we, too, will hear the music of David's harp."

And so it was that every night at midnight, during our stay in Jerusalem, we stood at the Wall and we heard David's song:

> One thing I ask of the L-rd, one thing I desire,
> to dwell in the house of the L-rd all the days of my
> life . . .

(Psalm 27:4)

It was midnight when we met a young soldier who had been among those who had liberated Jerusalem. He told us about his best friend who had fallen on the Temple Mount at the very spot where once, long ago, the altar had stood.

"I ran to my friend," he told us, "I tried to help him, but it was too late. I broke down and wept, and as I cried, I heard an eerie sound. It was the braying of a donkey echoing in the night. The donkey actually seemed to sob with me, crying in pain, as if imploring to be allowed to carry the Messiah into the Holy City."

The war lasted six days, and the seventh day was begging to come—the seventh day that is all Sabbath, the day that is Messiah.

Never before in the annals of mankind did a war last six days. But that too was preordained, for Jerusalem's reunification with her children was the prelude to *that seventh day*.

And for a very brief moment, it appeared as if our people might just understand and be prepared to respond to this awesome challenge. But all too soon, the magic of the moment evaporated.

The Six Day War was an open manifestation of the miracles of the Almighty. But we were loath to accept that which defies our intellectual scrutiny, and alas, the return of our people to Jerusalem took us unawares.

The moment came, and the moment passed, and the braying of the donkey was lost in the wind.

It is midnight at the Wall. The winds of Jerusalem are blowing. David's harp is playing, and G-d still waits for you and me to usher in that Seventh Day.

How can we usher in that Seventh Day?

By "turning the hearts of the fathers to their sons and the sons to their fathers" (*Malachi* 3:24), by becoming one with our families, and by kindling that precious Sabbath light through which each of us can find our way to G-d.

Temple Israel

Minneapolis, Minnesota

In Honor of the Bat Mitzvah of
ALEXIS IRENE PRASS
by her parents,
David and Suzanne Prass
June 18, 1983